WHAT OTH

MU00412489

I was privileged to read this book.

'Privileged' because rarely does one encounter a person that walks through an intense season of despair with authentic grace, raw vulnerability and honest humility.

The advice and insight Kirby gives in this book did not come cheaply. These priceless pearls of wisdom Kirby shares with us are hard-fought truths, gifted by her Creator. God chose to reward Kirby's living faith as she walked authentically through this trial. 'As' she walked it. Not, pretending that everything was ok, for it was most certainly not ok. Not, bemoaning the betrayal committed against her, and trying to enroll others into her misery. But by faithfully pressing into His grace and mercy and allowing Him to make her better if she resisted the understandable temptation to become bitter.

Since you've read this far, it may be because you've entered into a difficult season of your own. *Walking Through Fire Without Getting Burned* is a tremendous resource to take with you on your journey. It's filled with messages you need to hear - many are encouraging ones; others are hard truths that you need to face and accept. What you get from this book, and this journey you're on, will be directly proportional to what you bring to it. Let me encourage you to bring all of who you are to the Creator who loves you immeasurably more than you can ask or imagine.

When God led the Israelites out from Egypt into the desert to journey to the Promised Land, it could have been less than a two-week long walk. Instead, because of the hardness of their hearts and their response to Him during the season of trial, the journey lasted over 40 years! How you walk the path ahead, and how long it takes you to get to your own promised land, lies largely in your own hands. Take up your cross and walk the path laid out for you. Be sure you get the help you need along the way. What you hold in your hands at the moment will be a good start and a faithful companion as you travel.

—BRETT PYLE, FOUNDER OF CONNECTING PEOPLE TO THEIR PURPOSE

As a friend and a pastor, I have watched Kirby walk through very good days and very difficult days. Through her trials, I saw a sister in Christ who wanted to do things God's way over her way. Her wisdom comes from the Word and from her experience, and I pray that this book will help others as they endure through the fires that come their way.

—DR. TRAVIS AGNEW, PASTOR AND AUTHOR

Walking Through Fire Without Getting Burned offers hope for the believer who finds herself in the most wounded of places. With practical tips and suggested activities accompanying each chapter, *Walking Through Fire Without Getting Burned* continues to point the reader to Christ, encouraging her to seek His presence in the middle of the personal storm. Teaching what it means to truly abide in Christ, Kirby King then illustrates what it looks like to actively trust the 'lifter of our heads and the lover of our souls' with the pain involved in recovery from deep offense. Kirby effectively juxtaposes a Biblical perspective of handling personal storms over the humanistic attitude encouraged in today's culture. *Walking Through Fire Without Getting Burned* challenges the reader to find the "good" that God is up to in the darkest of personal circumstances, while strengthening her personal walk of faith, bringing glory and honor to the One called Redeemer. This book is a wonderful resource, designed for group study as well as individual.

—STEPHANIE BAKER, FOUNDER OF LIFE IN ABUNDANCE MINISTRIES,
  COUNSELOR & COACH

Thank you Kirby, for your beautiful gift of transparency. This book allows us to see what abiding in Christ looks like as you have had to walk through the fire that was trying to destroy you. Your deep bond of trust with God encourages each of us to hold on deeper to God. The words in this book bring hope. They show us how we too can abide in God even when our fires are raging. We *can* stay secure in Him and He *will* bring us through the fire.

—JOMARIE JOHANSON, CHRISTIAN LIFE COACH

Walking Through Fire Without Getting Burned helped me to see that I am not alone in my circumstances and others are walking through similar trials in their marriages. This book allowed me to have hope and healing and know that the Lord will continue to work in and through my life. My participation in the Walking Through Fire support group for women gave me the opportunity to sit side by side with others who needed support as I did. It created a safe place to talk with other women who understood what I had been through without judgment. I am so thankful that this book and group was available at just the right time for me.

-JENNIFER, PARTICIPANT IN WALKING THROUGH FIRE CLASS

I am so thankful for this book and the ability to study it with other like minded woman. I began the class thinking it was more of a "support group" to talk about being betrayed but quickly learned it was more about my relationship with God, which was exactly what I needed in order to walk through my fire. The things I have learned have literally changed my life. I have found a deep sense of joy that I never really understood before. Since going through the class six months ago, I have implemented journaling to God (my prayers, thoughts, songs, etc.), as Kirby suggested, and now also have a prayer partner, who has been an incredible source of encouragement. We look forward to our weekly, Tuesday morning prayer calls! These important steps have allowed me to have a relationship with God that I have not experienced before, though I have been a believer for 30+ years.

—H.W., PARTICIPANT IN WALKING THROUGH FIRE CLASS

Walking Through Fire Without Getting Burned is a lifesaving message showing how God is able to bring us through unexpected and difficult trials in life. Kirby King has provided a powerful testimony of faith in action with transparency and veracity. I was truly blessed as I read each invigorating chapter enriched with scriptures that strengthened my walk with the Lord. I laughed, I cried, I praised! You too will truly be blessed by the gift of hope beautifully unveiled in this book.

—VENUS DIXON, DIRECTOR OF RENEWAL CENTER (ADDICTION RECOVERY)

FINDING HOPE IN THE HARD PLACES

WALKING
THROUGH FIRE
Without
GETTING BURNED

Kirby King

Copyright © 2019 Kirby King

HopeforHardPlaces.com

All rights reserved. No part of this publication may be reproduced, stored in a retrieval system or transmitted, in any form or by any means, electronic, mechanical, recorded, photocopied, or otherwise, without the prior written permission of the copyright owner, except by a reviewer who may quote brief passages in a review.

Cover image by jonkmanphotography.com

ISBN: 978-0-578-51109-2 (print)

Contents

Introduction

Life sometimes brings us to an unexpected crossroads. That place where the familiar road we've been on comes to an abrupt stop. Here we are given an opportunity to choose which road we will take, or at least we choose how we will walk the road we've been put on. At this junction we realize that our life as we once knew it is about to change and will never be the same.

Walking Through Fire Without Getting Burned is a book I've written while standing at a crossroads in my marriage. A place, which for me, came from being continually betrayed. Each of us who stands at our personal crossroads must ask ourselves this.

How are we going to walk through the fire without being consumed?

Please understand that much of the book you are holding was written while still in the heat of the fire. Not knowing if my marriage, or I, could sustain such a blow. Throughout the writing of these chapters, still reeling from the impact, I could often feel a dangerous backdraft working to suck me back into places of despair.

Truly this is a battlefield. The promise found in the words from the prophet Isaiah is the first weapon of defense God gave me early on in those battle days. This is God's promise for you as well.

> "When you walk through the fire, you will not be burned; the flames will not set you ablaze" Isaiah 43:2.

I do not write with an expertise on how to counsel others in the fire. For I am still surrounded by smoldering embers that have come from watching 35 years of trust in my marriage go up in smoke. The smell of fumes are here, even now, waiting to suck the air back out of me. Yet I do write as someone who is learning to walk in trust and full surrender, walking closely with the Faithful One.

God doesn't want to see any marriage come to an end. It is not His best for His children. I believe that. So many questions. How does anyone ever find closure from a relationship to which you've devoted so much of your life? I have no desire to redefine myself and start over. How does anyone deal with so many unknowns? Unknowns like these:

- How might my financial needs be met this year, or the year after that?
- How do I balance a checkbook?
- How do I file for my own credit card when they're now in both our names?
- How do I get insurance and what kind am I supposed to get?
- How do I change the ink cartridge on the printer?
- How do I raise our children if we're not raising them together?
- How do I face my fears of being alone? And how do I define myself when it's just "me"?
- How do I ever forgive someone who has betrayed me to the core?

Little time has been spent planning for this unexpected place I now face. It's hard to plan for a future where you don't want to go. I certainly don't need to add any worries about days to come to *this* day. Today has enough worries of its own. All of these questions and uncertainties I honestly have no clue about. The thought of any one of them could consume me if I allow my mind to fixate there.

Today I am choosing not to obsess and worry. Instead I am

choosing to keep my eyes fixed on Jesus and keep calling out to Him. It is the only thing I know how to do. Making this choice at my crossroads is what drives me to share with you the powerful lessons I have learned. The purpose of this book is to equip each of us with tools to help us run to Jesus.

I don't know the details of your circumstances, but I feel your pain. And from this perspective, my hope is to empower you to walk through the fires of your life without getting burned. I pray that you will use each chapter of this book as a tested weapon of defense against the enemy's continual efforts to make you feel defeated. You are not.

Prepare to put on God's Word and walk in victory.

Chapter 1

FOR ALL OUR FIRES
HEALING STARTS WITH A PRAYER

Hear my prayer from months ago at what turned out to be the conception of this book:

> *Lord, I don't want to waste a tear, a lesson learned, or a hope gained. I want to use everything you're teaching me as You and I have walked these months together. Let me write out of obedience. Let me record and hold onto what You have already done on my behalf. Help me to pass on Your abundant grace to others who have to walk where I have been. I have indeed been through the fire and not been burned up. Lord, my feet are on the ground and I am still standing. Somehow, some way, I want to see good come from all of this. Help me keep my eyes fixed on you Jesus, the author of my faith. Father, give me your clarity and wisdom to be able to recall and record your provisions for me, so others may benefit. Amen.*

A BOOK IS CONCEIVED

Moments after I wrote this prayer in my journal, I started writing down some of the key points to which God was opening my eyes. Lessons I was learning over the past painful months. I was writing as fast as the Lord was bringing each of the topics to mind. It turned out they would be the chapter titles of this book.

God has no intentions of wasting a single experience He allows into our lives. Not for me. And not for you. There are lessons to be learned from any fire God allows His children to walk through. This is the beauty of trusting Him. He doesn't want my thoughts to run too far ahead. He wants my eyes to stay focused on Him and what He has for me in this moment. There is still much good in today. None of what has happened in my marriage has caught the Lord by surprise. He is with me now and His Word promises He will be with me in the days ahead. God is the Faithful One who will walk securely by your side as well.

SURRENDERED TRUST

"For I am the Lord, your God, who takes hold of your right hand and says to you, Do not fear; I will help you" (Isaiah 41:13).

This is a journey I would never have chosen. But choosing to walk in absolute surrendered trust is making all the difference. There is joy in finding God's purposes in our pain.

Lord, let us not waste any of the pain.

Chapter 2

IT HAS **EVERYTHING** TO DO WITH ABIDING

There is a certain point of view in which I am writing my "lessons learned through the fire". I write from the perspective of one who has known Jesus Christ as Lord and Savior for nearly 40 years. For me, this means I choose to believe God is sovereign and He is good. And I am not. I believe God loves me so much He sent his Son, Jesus, over 2000 years ago, to live a perfect life. And ultimately to sacrifice his perfect life on a cross for me. Because I believe Jesus rose again and defeated death, my own sins are now forgiven. His forgiveness allows me to enjoy fellowship with God today and forever, even after my life on earth is done. This is the gospel message.

IT HAS EVERYTHING TO DO WITH GOD
There are people in my life I love very much who don't believe like I do. They don't believe there is One who is in control in the midst of all life's chaos. Some "unbelievers" would say a Christian is someone who needs their faith as a crutch. They say we are weak people. It is not my goal to argue this, but to testify to what I know to be true for me. I have walked through the fire these past two

years. I have experienced lies, deceit, accusations, and betrayal in my marriage. Yet I am not consumed by the fire. Instead I am stronger than I was before. I feel empowered and incredibly blessed. And it has EVERYTHING to do with God.

Never before have I felt so beaten down and under attack. It is incredibly hard to be told by the person you trusted, who has now hurt you, that it is (somehow) your fault for the bad choices that person chose to make. Yet, I can honestly say I have never felt the presence of God in the way I have these past months. I am learning to walk more closely with the Lord. And He has chosen *not* to take me out of the "firestorm." Rather, He has extended His hand for me to take hold. God wraps his loving arms tightly and securely around me as we walk *together* through each trial.

A PICTURE OF ABIDING

This is a picture of what abiding in Christ looks like. It is because of my relationship with Him that I can say I walk today with *peace* and *hope* for good things to come (from Jeremiah 29:11). I believe people are desperate to know they are unconditionally loved and accepted. They long to experience a Heavenly Father they can trust and feel safe with.

My greatest desire for you is that our creator God would be the One you learn to run to. Not only in the storms of life when you feel overwhelmed by the "waves." But also the One you can enjoy doing life with, each and every day.

The Creator of it all has a divine plan for us. He will show us what to do, even when we are not able to see the steps ahead. We do not walk alone. His grace is fully sufficient for our every step and our every decision. You are God's prized possession and He delights in you! He desires intimacy with his children. This personal closeness with God begins when we

You are God's prized possession and He delights in you!

realize from where our source of abundant life comes. A fully satis-
fying and abundant life will *not* be found in any human being. Life
in abundance is found in loving God above all others.

CONVERSATIONS WITH GOD

James 4:8 tells us to *"come near to God and He will come near
to you."* Taking time to read the Bible on a regular basis helps
us understand who God is and how very much He loves us. As
I will talk about in Chapter 4, it has always helped me to "get
personal" with God by journaling. A conversation with God is ini-
tiated whenever I write my thoughts and needs and questions to
Him on paper. As we pray, we learn to hear God's voice. We begin
to recognize when it's God speaking to our heart and when it's not.
His voice always lines up with His Word, the Bible. God wants for
us, even in the midst of battle, to experience an abiding peace and
confidence. This comes from Him alone. The secret of our joy is a
right relationship with the Father, through Christ.

Elizabeth Elliot, a woman who tragically lost two husbands,
beautifully writes the following in her book, *Be Still My Soul.*
She says, "To walk with God is to walk by faith, to trust and obey
one day at a time, recognizing our never-ending need for grace."
Though we may be clueless about much, we can be certain of
God's faithfulness to pour out His grace and walk closely beside
us. God will never leave us. Yet *we* are often the ones who choose
to try and walk the road alone.

As we hand over our burdens to God, He will replace our
overwhelming feeling of responsibility with an awareness of His
Presence. God places His strength and power inside of us when we
trust and release our fears to Him. He strengthens us as we surrender
our will to Him and follow His lead. This is abiding in Christ.

Be still and listen to the Father. There is a reason your heart
"wants" more. He made each and every one of us with a void
inside, which only He can fill. No matter the size of your void

today, God is able. I know this to be true. We learn His voice when we spend time with Him—and talk to Him in prayer.

MY PRAYER FOR YOU

Whether or not you are a believer in Christ, this is my heartfelt prayer for you. I pray the lessons I'm learning in this journey of mine will be a source of strength and blessing to you. I pray you will not allow your trials to burn you, but will choose the "high" road with God and allow Him to use the flames you find yourself in to make you *even better*. You deserve God's best!

Chapter 3

LEAVE NO STONE UNTURNED: CHOOSE RECONCILIATION

But I tell you that anyone who is angry with his brother will be subject to judgment...therefore, if you are offering your gift at the altar and there remember that your brother has something against you, leave your gift there in front of the altar. First go and be reconciled to your brother; then come and offer your gift.
MATTHEW 5:22-24

CONFRONTATION - GOD'S PERSPECTIVE

Here is a passage of Scripture which may push some of us beyond what we think we are capable of doing. Confrontation. Honestly, the idea of standing up to someone I had an issue with once made me feel sick inside. Literally. My preference was to try and ignore a repeated offense. This often caused resentment inside me to fester. Only recently have I begun to understand God's perspective of how to deal with controversy. To confront someone with whom we have an issue is a biblical command. And when done in love, and with pure motives, it is God's BEST for us.

How many times over the years have I run from the call to go and make things right? How many times have I run away from it because of my fear, stubbornness, and pride? For those who like to be in control, it's especially difficult. We don't know how the other person will respond to us. Taking our concerns to them could make the problem even worse.

WHO IS AT FAULT IS NOT AS IMPORTANT

There is an amazing beauty in Matthew's words in the above passage. In this scripture, there is no mention of the other person's response of our efforts to reconcile. Nor does Matthew find it important to include *who* is at fault in the matter at hand. Because who is at fault is not nearly as important as getting things right. This Scripture doesn't address the actions of the mentioned "brother." Instead, the verse speaks to the believer who stands before God desiring to worship Him. It urges you and me to do what it takes to make our hearts right with God. When we sense there is an offense between ourselves and someone else, we must go.

To *"go and be reconciled"* takes an incredible amount of trust in the One who is sending you. God may be asking you right now to go and do your part by attempting to make things right with your spouse. We will talk at great length in a later chapter about forgiveness and repentance. The focus here is to understand this: No matter how hard it may be, trying to reconcile and restore what has been broken is worth it. It is worth it to stand before God at the end of our days without regret.

> **It is worth it to stand before God at the end of our days without regret.**

It is worth it to know you were obedient in going to your brother, your sister, your spouse, to do what is right.

IT'S WORTH YOUR EFFORT TO BE SET FREE

It is worth all your efforts in order to have your heart set free. Free knowing that you have "left no stone unturned." Free because you did all you believed God put on your heart to do to make matters right. The outcome is not in your hands to control. Being obedient to go, and thus have your heart right before God, is in your hands. Matters unresolved are fertile ground for bitterness and anger and resentment. Do not give these things a foothold. They are negative emotions which will hinder your relationship with God and your enjoyment of Him.

IS THIS YOUR CROSSROADS?

So do you find yourself at a crossroads? The place where the rubber meets the road as to how you will choose to walk through your conflict? Try and take a good look down both roads. The road of working towards reconciliation or the road of choosing not to try? Which path do you believe will have the most eternal value? Listen to what the Lord says to us in Jeremiah 6:16. *"Stand at the crossroads and look...ask where the good way is, and walk in it, and you will find rest for your souls."*

The following is one of my favorite promises in all of Scripture. It's a promise to each of us God has our circumstances in His control. He sees all roads before us. When our eyes and ears are on Him, He will show us what to do. *"Whether you turn to the right or to the left, your ears will hear a voice behind you, saying, 'This is the way, walk in it' "*(Isaiah 30:21). Read that again, out loud, and hear with confidence that God will show you your path.

PRAYER: GOD HELP ME IN MY UNBELIEF

Lord Jesus, you know the ache in my heart, the longing for something I do not have in my marriage. Your Word says that I am to ask for whatever I wish in Jesus' name. It says if my asking is in line with Your will, then You will give what I ask. Am I understanding this right or have I missed it? Is it your desire, Your plan for a husband and wife to love each other? Respect each other? Enjoy intimacy with one another? Is it your desire that my husband would love me like Christ loved the church?

Then God, please help me not to give up hoping and longing. For when I do, I cannot bear it. I have to have hope. So Father, in the name of Jesus, through whom all things are possible, help me in my unbelief. Help me in my doubting and my feelings of hopelessness and despair. Give me hope that it will not always be like this. Give me hope that how we communicate with each other will one day be much better. Tender and gentle. Jesus, may Your light permeate our thinking. Fill us with life and peace. This is a scary place to be. God pull us out of it, please. I want to quit. To retreat and to curl up in a corner and let this painful life pass by. Lord, help me to want what You want.

"May the Lord make your love increase and overflow for each other" (1 Thessalonians 3:12).

PRAYER: I'M PREPARED TO DO FIERCE BATTLE

Father, glorify yourself through this very difficult valley our marriage is in right now. May You receive all the glory and praise in restoring what has been broken. Do this through whatever means You choose. Bring healing to our marriage. Draw us closer to each other and closer to You. Closer than we have ever been before. Open our eyes and our hearts to following You in this difficult time. Please don't let my heart grow cold toward my husband. Protect it, yet tender it to him.

Open my eyes, Lord, to how I can love my husband better. Show me how I can build him up. Protect my heart as I am in this vulnerable place. Lord, I will trust You in this. I am not giving up. I am doing, and will do, fierce battle. I will do whatever it takes to fight for my marriage and for my man. This is Your will and You will make a way. I am thanking You now, in advance, for the wonderful things You are about to do. Soon Lord. You are a God of miracles and we need a miracle. We need healing and a new direction. Soon. Amen.

PRAYER: DO YOUR WORK IN US, LORD

God, I am confident we will make it through, if our eyes stay focused on You. We can make it through this season. Open our eyes to see what it is You are doing. Working things through would be my preferred way end this very difficult, painful season we've been in. It could be a time we both learn to trust You more completely and to love each other more deeply. Lord, do Your work in us so others may see Your power of resurrection. May this marriage, which is dead to the life You desire for us as a couple, become alive again. May our marriage be filled with the newness of all things good and honorable. I love You, Lord. I love my husband.

PRAYER: DO NOT LET THE ENEMY GET HIS GRIP ON US

Guard our hearts Lord, especially during these extra difficult months. Help us to keep our focus on You and on the well-being of one another. Help us as we walk painfully through the consequences of our sin. Bring us joyfully to the other side of this, Lord. Please don't let us call it quits simply because it is too uncomfortable. Don't let the enemy get his grip on either one of us. For we can do all things You are asking us to do, through Christ who gives us strength.

For me, it was overwhelming to experience those days of emotional exhaustion. I felt numb, spent and unsettled. My heart feared moving forward in any attempt to put back together what looked to be shattered. Being willing to allow my heart to try to love and receive love again troubled me so much I felt ill.

Over and over there were new crossroads. Do we pursue additional counseling? Do I make myself vulnerable to his counselor who has a different perspective on things than mine? Do we commit to the expense and energy of an in-depth, overnight marriage intensive?

Each of these decisions overwhelmed me — *if* I lost sight of the One who walked closely beside me.

ASK GOD TO GIVE YOU CLARITY

The only step I was certain about was writing out each question in a prayer to the Lord. I asked God to grant me full clarity in my thinking and in all decisions I needed to make. I begged God to shut down completely any thoughts not in line with His path for me. I took the time to be still and to listen. I asked for His blessings on my steps. And I walked in the way I believed He was leading me.

God is not a God of confusion. He is a God of clarity. He just often chooses to speak in whispers that can only be heard in our hearts when we are still. *"In repentance and rest is your salvation. In quietness and trust is your strength"* (Isaiah 30:15).

A PROFOUND PRAYER FROM A FRIEND

Kirby, may God give you absolute clarity and divine discernment so you can see things as they are, and not as they seem. May He keep you far from accusing tongues and protect you from being wrongly assessed. May you have the backbone and conviction to stand up for what is true and to stand back when God wants to fight for you. May God give you laser-like focus to tend to your God-given assignments. May your pure heart and firm faith keep you steady on the path ahead of you. These things are yours because you belong to Him. Be strong and courageous today. Amen.

These words, given to me by a friend in my hour of need, made a deep impression on my heart and gave me the clarity I needed.

How grateful I am when the Lord speaks to my heart. The following is God's gentle answer to my persistent question, "What am I to do next?" *Kirby, My daughter, this is not what selfishness looks like. Your obeying My leading does not have to feel "bad" to be okay. It is I AM who gives you the peace and joy right now. When you muddle in delayed obedience you lose My peace. Know this is from Me. When it is well with your soul you should trust that My Spirit is walking closely with you. Rest in this. Keep your eyes fixed on Me. Stand still and let Me fight for you. You need only to stand. Trust and see that I AM is good. I love you.*

"Forget the former things; do not dwell on the past. See I am doing a new thing! Now it springs up; do you not see it? I am making a way in the desert and streams in the wasteland" (Isaiah 43:18-19).

Chapter 4

BREATHE AND TRUST:
ACKNOWLEDGE
YOUR DESPERATION

I have been learning that my times of desperation need not be seen as times of weakness. Rather, a time of resolute surrender. God tells us in 2 Corinthians 12:9-10 that His power is made perfect in our weakness. He says we are to *"delight in weaknesses, in insults, in hardships, in persecutions, in difficulties. For when I am weak then I am strong."* I am to acknowledge my desperation and need of a greater source of help outside myself. This is what God desires most from all His children. He wants us to offer to Him a complete surrender of our own will. It is by His design that we seek the Lord in our times of despair.

I have cried out to the Lord. And what my heart has heard Him say over and over to me is this: "Breathe and Trust." "Breathe and Trust." I slow my breathing and my thinking down with a long, deep breath. And I allow the stress and worries in my head to release while slowly exhaling my breath. Then I find I'm much more prepared to redirect my focus away from me, and onto my Savior. Sometimes, as I quiet my mind before Him, my heart hears

His voice. In those moments, He seems to speak words of comfort so clearly. The following are a few of those special moments when I felt God speak to my heart.

NEEDED WORDS FROM THE FATHER

Child, I delight in you no matter what. No matter if you work and serve, read, pray, run, walk, or lose it. My love for you does not change or lessen. Delight in Me. Enjoy Me in your day-to-day adventures. Be joyous in your day. For you are mine. You belong to the Creator of the Universe, who knows you, hears you, and speaks to you.

MY GRACE IS SUFFICIENT

Daughter, BREATHE Me in each morning, and let that be the breath which sustains you through the remainder of the day. Lay your cares down at my feet. Leave them with Me and find great rest in knowing that your Father has things under control. Yes, My grace is sufficient to meet ALL your needs. It is sufficient to carry you through the green pastures. As well as through the fiery trials, so you will not be burned up.

Hope in Me. Believe that the path I have you on today is a good one. Find delight in ME—not the path—during each day. BREATHE, laugh, learn. Be gentle with yourself, and your family. Love well and extend much grace. Remember, I am going to fill you with sufficient grace day after day, moment by moment. Just as you need it. Do not fear. My grace and goodness are not going to run out. It is by design, My design, that you seek Me in desperation. I will not disappoint. Desperation for Me and My ways is never a sign of weakness. Rather surrender, which is what I desire most.

FIND JOY IN THESE MOMENTS

Precious one, I love you just where you are in your journey with Me. I love you. My Spirit delights in you because I created you, and My work is good. Find joy in these moments I am giving you. Find joy in these people I place in your path. Splash joy on them. Listen, laugh, encourage, and pray for others. Know that what you do, whatever you do in My name, is good. Be a blessing.

Not one of the experiences we have walked through together, good or "bad," is meant to be wasted. I have filled you with My wisdom and discernment. I have filled you with My Spirit. All for My purposes. Delight in being used by Me in the small moments. Tenderness will come from Me. A warmness of heart and emotions will be poured out by Me when you surrender the desire you have to control and to fix. Let it go.

THIS IS MY GIFT FOR YOU

Beloved, find contentment in times of great frustration. Every moment of your "exasperation" is a beautiful reminder of your need for Me. This, precious child, is My gift to you. Because in your need, you will not forget Me. Delight in that! Each "overwhelming" morning or afternoon with your children is an opportunity to bow before Me. It is an opportunity to re-prioritize our relationship and allow Me to lead and supply all your needs.

When I am the One who meets your needs, others will see this. They will see you have been with Jesus and they will want what you have. They will want this peace which passes all understanding. Trust Me. Love Me. Let yourself, My daughter, be drenched in my love.

LET ME FIGHT THIS BATTLE FOR YOU

Child, what has happened to you is not a surprise to Me. Watch and see what I am doing and be amazed in Me. TRUST and obey. Trust and BREATHE, and let Me show you the joy in the moments, these moments. There is joy because I am fully here with you.

Child, never forget that your intimacy with Me is where and how you find strength. It is God's power that indwells you. Not your own. *Be prepared every day, especially when you are tired, to put your spiritual armor in place. Let Me fight this battle for you. BREATHE and TRUST. Maintain your integrity no matter what. This may require a greater degree of trust and faith than you have ever known.*

BE STILL AND KNOW

Daughter, be still and know that I AM God. I am He, and there is no other. BREATHE and TRUST and BREATHE and TRUST. Continue to do this until I return. I have got this and I have got you. And I AM is good. I love you more than you can fathom. Indeed My plans are to prosper you and yours. Not to harm you. This has always been My plan.

I want you to TRUST Me and my timing. I want you to learn to be still and to worship Me in the wait. For in the wait, you will know Me. Hear my whisper. Watch for my hand. I am moving on your behalf. In quietness and TRUST is your strength. BREATHE.

Chapter 5

DO I HAVE TO JOURNAL?
IT'S A DIALOGUE
BETWEEN YOU AND GOD

Are you upset? Confused? Angry? Overwhelmed? Or is it well with your soul today? Write it down. Express yourself on paper. Don't hold back. This isn't just a therapeutic exercise on paper.

This is a dialogue between you and the Lord.

This is your opportunity to connect with the Creator of the Universe. This is where you record your conversations with God.

You know who our best teacher is on how to express ourselves through journaling? King David. He along with other psalmists give us 150 chapters in the book of Psalms as models for us to follow. David has taught me that it is acceptable, and even healthy at times, to "let it all hang out" with my words to the Lord. David wasn't ashamed to praise and adore his Lord. Nor was he ashamed to cry out and plead with Him. God was never offended by David's doubts, fears, or complaints. Reading the psalms gives us permission to cry out to God. They let us know it's okay to express our frustration and ask questions of the Lord. It's okay even to grumble. As long as it is prayerfully directed to God (and not to others). This is good news when your mind is full of thoughts and emotions that need a healthy place to be released! Even better, once these emotions *are* laid to rest on paper, you are less likely to feel you have to hold on to them inside.

USE THE PSALMS TO HELP YOU WORSHIP - PART

For nearly 20 years I have used the Psalms to help me begin my morning time of devotion with the Lord. Becky Tirabassi has a wonderful book called, *Let Prayer Change Your Life,* which taught me how to get started. She suggests an acronym which serves to lead people into the presence of the Lords, and into His Holy of Holies. The acronym is PART. It is similar to the ACTS (Adoration, Confession, Thanksgiving, Supplication) acronym of prayer that many are familiar with, but hers has more detail.

The P in PART stands for Psalms. We can praise God through the Psalms. Begin your devotion by writing out one of the psalms in your own words. Paraphrase it, using pronouns such as I, me, my and so on.. For example, let's look at Psalm 46. It says, "God is our refuge and strength, an ever-present help in trouble. Therefore we will not fear, though the earth give way..." Personalize the words and write to God, saying something like this: *God, You are my refuge and my strength today. You have always been there in the past to help me in my troubles and You will be there for me today. I will not be afraid. God, please help me today not to be afraid.* Psalms 18, 23, 27, 30, 34, and 40 are particularly good ones to start with.

A in PART stands for Admit. Admit your sins before the Lord. It's important for us to approach God with a clear conscience in order to experience His presence.

Ask God to show you what your part has been in your marriage relationship being where it is today. Own up to where you may have been at fault and admit those things to God. He is eager to forgive.

R is for Request. This is your time to ask God for help in anything you want to bring to Him. Sometimes I will write out people's names for whom I'm praying. Then I will jot words such as comfort, protection, or joy to help me focus my prayers for each person. Other times, if I am particularly burdened to pray, I may write out a page or more, Being very specific with every detail of my request. Then when lying in bed at night, when "worries" creep back into play, I remind myself that those concerns have already been brought to the Lord. They have already been laid at the feet of Jesus who hears my prayers. This helps me do a better job of quickly giving my concerns back to God and keeping my eyes focused on Him. These written requests will serve as reminders to me later, of God's faithfulness when I read back through my journal.

Finally, **T stands for Thanksgiving.** We can never thank God enough. I will talk more about telling God what we are thankful for in the *Count Your Blessings* chapter. Everyone appreciates a thank you note. Especially God!

SEE THE FINGERPRINT OF GOD

Writer and pastor, Chuck Swindoll, calls journaling a "spiritual diary where you record God's activity in your life. A place where you are able to see the fingerprint of God in your life." I have found this to be true. Much of this, *Walking Through Fire* book is taken from the journals I have kept over the past two years. I journaled it all as a prayer while walking through the fire of my marriage falling apart.

NO NEED TO APOLOGIZE - GOD'S NOT OFFENDED

There are many benefits which accompany the discipline of prayer journaling. One is the safety of expressing myself on paper in a prayer. I am free to write whatever is on my heart. In all its rawness, I can tell God what makes me angry or anxious or sad. I never need to apologize to my Heavenly Father—God already knows what I'm thinking. He is able to identify with what I am feeling. And He is patient enough to love me through every one of my emotions. I am safe with Him.

This is in stark contrast to me venting my frustrations on Facebook or some other form of social media. There I might write or say something I may later regret. I might say something which slanders someone else or tarnishes Christ in me. Why not run to my best friend, Jesus, instead? When life seems too much to bear, I express my struggles in a "Dear God" letter. I never need to feel bad for "bothering Him" one more time. He wants me to come to Him. If I need to express my frustrations, God can handle it. He's not offended. And He's a great listener.

DO NOT TAKE THE BAIT!

John Bevere, in his book *Bait of Satan*, says that Satan's bait is to offend. To offend is a verb meaning to cause to feel upset, annoyed, or resentful. Someone's words or actions to me, which cause me to be offended, are not themselves harmful or destructive. They're only harmful if I *choose* to pick those words up and internalize them. This is what happens when I take "the bait" and allow myself to be offended. This is what happens when I let the offense fester and brew in my mind. Bevere says much bad fruit is produced. Fruit "such as hurt, anger, outrage, jealousy, resentment, strife, bitterness, hatred, and envy."

These emotions are in direct contrast to the fruit produced when I allow the Holy Spirit to take control of my thoughts. Fruit such as *"love, joy, peace, patience, kindness, goodness, faithfulness, gentleness, self control"* (Galatians 5:22 NASB). So the question is this: The next time you and I are offended by someone, what will our *response* be to that offense?

One response might be to write these feelings down. Some people prefer to keep a record of their life events and the things God is teaching them separate from their actual prayer journal. My mind isn't that organized. I find myself in the middle of paraphrasing one of the Psalms and I think of a prayer request that can't wait to be recorded. Or I think of a praise I want to include under "Blessings," which I record in the back. I have chosen to use my journal to write it all down. I write my notes from Sunday sermons and Bible study, my conversations with God and His answers. I write prayer requests and "Blessings." It's all in my journal. I encourage you to find a method that works for you, and continue to work at it. It's a discipline worth your effort.

HEAR MY PRAYERS, LORD - I CAN'T DO THIS ALONE

Lord, how do I put into words this hurt? Jesus, I know that I am nowhere big enough to bear this alone. The emotional pain feels unbearable. Be my hope and my reason to move forward. Help me to live today, these next hours, trusting You and speaking and acting as someone who trusts. I give You all of this, Jesus. I give You my hurts, my husband, and my future. I ask You to make much good of this mess. Jesus, be in me and for me what I cannot be. Be my rock, my fortress, my strong tower, my anchor, my salvation. I am wounded, Father.

Father, what are the desires of my heart? Sometimes I feel like I haven't any, except to get through the next day. I don't want to be like this. I want to experience life abundantly, to the fullest. Sometimes I don't feel as if You are sufficient to care for all my needs, Lord. And this fills me with fear. Sometimes I really don't believe I can make it through these circumstances. This isn't true. Help me with my fears. Help me to know I can do all things through Christ who gives me strength. Amen.

And Jesus Christ says to all of us: *"In this world you will have trouble. But take heart! I have overcome the world"* (John 16:33).

Chapter 6

ARE YOU BATTLING THE ENEMY? PRAY! MAKE YOUR DOWN A BOW DOWN

I heard Beth Moore speak on prayer at a conference I attended. She said that when we bow down in prayer, we rob the enemy of the defeat we often experience from those things that bring us down. Our "down" becomes a BOW DOWN. Something that takes us to our knees. We declare that God is Lord over whatever has gotten us down. Being on our knees in prayer, she said, is to be the "new bottom which will keep us from free falling with the enemy."

I don't know if you can identify with "free falling with the enemy," but I can. I can hear his lies in my head of how worthless I am and how hopeless my situation is. And for a moment, I allow myself to agree. For a moment the gravity of my situation has me ready to throw in the towel and quit. But in a "Bow Down" you can picture the heaviness inside you as a God-ordained weight. A weight which drops you down on your knees. We cannot assume a more powerful posture than bowing to receive strength from the Lord. For from *this* place, the real battle has just begun.

WE NEED A WAR ROOM

"For the eyes of the Lord range throughout the earth to strengthen those whose hearts are fully committed to him" (2 Chronicles 16:9). Therefore, commit yourself to pray often. If you can get your hands on a copy of the *War Room* DVD, it is so worth the watch. There is a powerful scene where the viewer gets a look into the prayer closet of Miss Clara. Miss Clara is a faithful prayer warrior who understands that *"our struggle is not against flesh and blood, but against the rulers, against the authorities, against the powers of this dark world and against the spiritual forces of evil in the heavenly realms"* (Ephesians 6:12).

Our battles cannot be fought using only human resources. We need a means of obtaining much more ammunition with which to fight. Miss Clara's "war room" is an empty closet. Empty except for a chair and four walls covered with post-it notes filled with names and prayers—prayers for the people she is committed to do spiritual battle for. Regularly she sits alone in her prayer closet and prays aloud with expectancy to the Lord. She is interceding for these people's needs. Miss Clara's advice? "Ask God for what you need. Take your time and then you listen."

Yes ma'am! I wish I could say that I spent as much time in my prayer closet as Miss Clara. I'm a work in progress. Scripture reminds us *"you do not have, because you do not ask God"* (James 4:2). God wants us to ask Him for the things we need. Whether we ask Him out loud, in our hearts, or in written prayers, He wants us to ask.

GOD, I FEEL NO HOPE

Here is how I asked God for help when the weight of it all had brought me to my knees. *Help me, Jesus. I am asking You. Fill me with Your hope and Your peace that surpasses all my understanding. Fill me with Your joy and love, Your grace and mercy. Fill me with Your patience and long-suffering in all my trials. For I have run out completely. Fill me with kindness and self control. God I need You. I am empty. I feel no hope. I am incredibly discouraged, sad, and at the end of myself. Jesus, be faith and hope in me today. Lift me up and out of this miry pit. Help me to not only believe, but to feel Your compassion and Your faithfulness for me today. Help me to wait with a great hope and an eager anticipation for wonderful things to come from You. Amen.*

One friend suggests using 3 x 5 cards to write the name and prayer requests (with the date requested) on each card. She then adds to those requests as needed. This friend keeps these cards bound together so she can work through her cards, praying for specific needs. If keeping prayer cards with you in your purse or car encourages you to pray, great. If putting written prayers on the wall as a visual reminder helps, then go for it. Whatever works best for you. The point is to pray.

It always makes me smile when I can read back over a list of prayer requests and see God's hand at work. I get to see the way He's already answered many of my prayers. Often I've already forgotten I even asked God for His help. Writing down my requests helps me remember.

FIND A PRAYER PARTNER

Find yourself a prayer partner. Be wise in choosing the friend to whom you'll entrust your more intimate prayer needs. You want her to be a woman of integrity who can be trusted to keep your requests confidential and be faithful to intercede on your behalf. For me, it's important that this person will allow me the privilege of sharing her burdens in prayer as well. One of the dangers of being forced to walk "through the fire" for months at a time is that your focus can easily get stuck on your own struggles and nothing else. I am forever grateful for my friends who pray me through the harder days, yet on my stronger days, allow me to ask how I can pray for them.

Know this. The enemy is a stalker who is coming after you and the ones you care for. He has no greater desire than to tear apart your marriage and to make you ineffective in serving the Lord. He can use your mistakes and your feelings of shame to make you think you shouldn't come to God with your needs.

ARE YOU FASTER TO TEXT OR TO PRAY?

So often I get caught up in the struggles of my day and forget that I can bring each one of my troubles to the Lord in prayer. An offensive word can be said that catches me off guard. Or a text shows up on my phone that upsets me. My emotions then begin to drive my thinking. It's exhausting and unproductive. Worry takes over which gets me nowhere (except for a headache and diarrhea). Sometimes I am faster to call or text a friend with my troubles than I am to pray. I am faster to worry than to close my eyes and say, *Jesus, help me. I don't know what to do.* I want to be in the habit of going to the Lord first.

Our strongest offensive weapon against the enemy is the Word of God. Spiritual battles need spiritual weaponry. Ephesians 6:17 calls God's Word *"the sword of the Spirit."*

GET OUT YOUR SWORD

So what might it look like to fight our battles holding God's Word out as a sword? Your sword may be a 3 x 5 card ready to pull from your pocket with these words on it: *"I can do everything through Christ, who gives me strength"* (Philippians 4:13 NLT). Speaking truth aloud when frustrations hit is powerful. It may be this verse taped to your bathroom mirror: *"If God is for us, who can be against us?"* (Romans 8:31) Here's a verse that has helped me many times when my thoughts are taking me to a place I don't need to go: *"Whatever is true, whatever is noble, whatever is right, whatever is pure, whatever is lovely, whatever is admirable...think about such things...and the God of peace will be with you"* (Philippians 4:8-9).

When reading this verse, I literally stop at each word and make a mental list of those things in my life that are *true*. And those things around me that are noble and pure. Taking the time to work through the apostle Paul's list never fails to change my thinking. These words move me away from my former mindset, the one that had my mind in a bad place. Focusing on Scripture moves our thinking onto a more righteous path.

I keep a stack of 3 x 5 cards, filled with some of my favorite verses, in the side pocket of my car. When the enemy hits me with his tactics of worry and anger, I whip out my sword (my stack of Bible verses) and start fighting back. I speak God's Word with authority over the enemy and can see the enemy for what he really is. He is a pathetic wimp who loses his "oomph" when I speak Scripture to him. I have quit being concerned that onlookers from other cars may think I have lost my marbles. Who cares? I have more important business to take care of.

Seeing the power of fighting battles by praying Scripture aloud should encourage each one of us to try and be more disciplined. It's worth the effort to commit to memory as much of God's word as we can. We never know where we may find ourselves when we need to pull out our Sword and fight. Or which verses we might need that pertain to the battle we find ourselves in. If you don't know a Scripture that speaks to your specific struggle, ask a friend. Ask her to help you find a verse that fits. Then write it out. Study and digest it. Memorize it and claim it as yours.

WE NEVER NEED TO FIGHT ALONE

Never do we fight alone when we call on God to fight our battles for us. We can find comfort in knowing Romans 8:26. When we don't know *how* to pray or even *what* to ask God for, He has us covered. This verse tells us His Spirit, which lives in every believer, will intercede to the Father on our behalf. God knows our hearts.

When I asked friends for their suggestions on ways that help them pray more effectively, one praying friend shared this. "If I am feeling fear, or rejection, or I can't think clearly, I literally stop and pull my car over wherever I am. I stop and ask the Lord for peace. Peace to know He is in this, and I am not alone. I ask for reassurance to know He is faithful and true. I ask for a reminder that my trust is in Him." She says she has to take the time to do this. She waits until the peace comes back. Then she can go about her day. This friend sees praying without ceasing as the lifeline available to sustain each one of us. I couldn't agree more.

When we open our hands and offer up our struggles to the Lord. When we ask Him to help us. This increases our ability to receive His answers and blessings. Here is an example of me asking. *God, keep my head clear so I can get the counsel I need and make the wisest decisions for my family. This is not the life I thought I would be living. This is not what I hoped for or could ever have imagined. Lord, help me to live and to act as a human being who is worthy of respect. Because I am. Guard my heart from breaking. Yet do not let it be hardened to love. Please give me clarity to know how long I am to keep fighting for my marriage. Amen.*

We are to ask, in faith, with our whole heart's desire.

God wants us to ask with an eager anticipation that He will answer. When we limit our asking and expectation of God, we may limit what we will receive. We are to ask, in faith, with our whole heart's desire. Don't hold back. We need clarity in our asking, not because our heavenly Father doesn't know what it is we need (He does), but for us to better be able to receive. When Jesus asked the paralytic at the pool *"Do you want to be healed?"* (John 5:6 ESV), He wanted the man to acknowledge his need for help, and to be sure that the man truly wanted to be healed.

WHAT DO YOU WANT GOD TO DO FOR YOU?

Sometimes I feel I can hear the Lord ask me, *Kirby, what do you want Me to do for you?* Am I just grumbling because it feels good to grumble or do I really want God to intervene? When my eyes are focused only on my earthly concerns, I miss the prayers He is answering. I miss the blessings He showers on me throughout the day.

Abba Father, my daddy, hold me close. Please hold me. Protect me and my family through this fire so we will not be burned up. And God hears my prayer and gently answers, *Precious child, keep your eyes upward. Keep them heavenly sighted. Let Me rain down. Let Me pour out my Spirit, My solutions and blessings onto you. Be ready to receive. Ask expectantly. For I can do more than you can ever ask or imagine.*

The Psalmist knew where his strength came from. *"I sought the Lord and He answered me; He delivered me from all my fears. Those who look to Him are radiant, their faces are never covered in shame"* (Psalm 34:4-5).

Chapter 7

GOD, WHAT DO I DO NEXT? THE BIBLE IS A SAFE PLACE TO SEEK COUNSEL

The Bible is God's blueprint for how we are to build our lives. Since He "created my inmost being" and "knit me together in my mother's womb" (Psalm 139:13), then it only makes sense that God would have some written instructions as a guide for making me into what He created me to be. The Bible is our heavenly Father's love letter to us, His children. Since *"All Scripture is God-breathed and is useful for teaching, rebuking, correcting and training in righteousness so that the man of God may be thoroughly equipped for every good work"* (2 Timothy 3:16-17), then truly the Word of God is a wonderful and safe place for us to seek counsel. The Bible's teaching shows us the path we're to go on. It's rebuking shows us where we got off the path of godly living. It's correcting tells us how to get back on that path. And its training teaches us how to stay on the path.

Get into God's Word.

Even if it has not been the place where you have spent much time in the past, today is a new day. Open your bible and read it. Read it again tomorrow and then the next. Read the Word every day. Remember that you are not alone as you open up the Word of God. *"If any of you lacks wisdom, he should ask God, who gives generously to all without finding fault, and it will be given him"* (James 1:5).

Don't be intimidated or overwhelmed by the words you don't understand. The Holy Spirit longs to speak to you through the Scriptures. Ask Him to give meaning to your reading, and to show you how to apply God's truth to what you are going through right now. Get yourself into a Bible study which will help hold you accountable to stay in the Word. Many churches have ongoing Bible study groups which meet weekly during the day or evenings. Tell a friend that you are trying to become more disciplined in reading your Bible and ask her to pray for you and hold you accountable.

BE QUIET AND LET GOD SPEAK TO YOU

Impressed on my heart from the Lord one evening was this. It was a reminder of where my strength should come from: *Kirby, be quiet now. No more expression. Let Me speak to your heart and impress My words on you. Be still and know today that I am God. Child, I've got this. I care about you. I care that you, a server of your family, a stay at home mom, get to experience Me in real and powerful ways. Continue to seek Me and My ways. I have so much more for you to see and experience. It is not always My will for others around you to see My hand in miraculous ways. Enjoy Me as I delight in you.*

COUNSEL IN THE PSALMS

Reading through the Psalms is a beautiful place to find comfort and strength. Let's look at Psalm 18 as an example. The first three verses reflect on God's attributes:

> I love you, O Lord, my *strength*. The Lord is my *rock*, my *fortress* and my *deliverer*, my God is my rock, in whom I

take *refuge*. He is my *shield* and the *horn of my salvation*, my *stronghold*. I call to the Lord who is worthy of praise, and I am saved from my enemies .

In verse 6, the psalmist shows us what we're to do in our time of need:

In my distress *I called to the Lord; I cried to my God for help*. From his temple He heard my voice; my cry came before Him, into his ears [emphasis mine].

Now be encouraged by reading what God does in verses 14-19, for the one who called out to Him for help:

He reached down from on high and *took hold of me;* he *drew me out* of deep waters. He *rescued me* from my powerful enemy, from my foes, who were too strong for me. They confronted me in the day of my disaster, but *the Lord was my support*. He brought me out into a spacious place; he rescued me because *he delighted in me* [emphasis mine].

Just like God Almighty provided for and equipped the writers of psalms years ago, He will do the same for you and me:

It is God who arms me with strength and makes my way perfect...He enables me to stand on the heights. He trains my hands for battle; my arms can bend a bow of bronze. You give me your shield of VICTORY [emphasis mine], and your right hand sustains me; You stoop down to make me great (vs. 32-35).

That's good stuff. And there are 149 more chapters in the Book of Psalms we can glean from!

USE YOUR BIBLE CONCORDANCE

Many chapters of the book you're now reading began with my own search through the Scriptures to see what God had to say about various issues in which I needed clarity: *Trust, Worry, our Tongue, Praise, Forgiveness,* and so on. Peacemaker was a topic I had a lot of questions about, so I spent much time digging there. The concordance of my NIV Study Bible has 95 verse references that have the word Peace, Peaceable, Peaceful, Peacemakers in them. I looked up the ones I thought might relate to my questions and struggles, and recorded in my prayer journal those verses which spoke to me. I would ask God, "What do You want me to get from these passages?" Often I would take a highlighter and mark keywords which helped me to better see patterns of God's repeated instruction and promises.

Many times we pass right over the meat of God's Word because it may contain a word we typically don't use (slander, shrewd, malice…). So if I ran across a word whose meaning was unclear to me, I looked it up in a dictionary and wrote down those meanings as well. Find a Bible with a good concordance in the back and do your own search. There is no other book that comes close to the Bible's power and influence. That's because it contains not only wise words, but the very living breath of God. Breath which waits to fill your heart and soul in a way you have never experienced before. When I experience days of "smooth sailing" with no particular struggles, I read God's Word with a limited appetite. However, when my days are full of troubles and darkness and uncertainties, I read with a desperateness to receive hope and guidance from the Lord. The greater our hunger for truth, the more of God we can expect to find. He wants to be found.

GOD, SHOW ME WHAT I NEED TO DO NEXT

God is not a God of confusion, but a God of clarity. Yes, He often has us seek and wait for His answers, but He *will* answer. *"Whether you turn to the right or to the left, your ears will hear a voice behind you, saying, 'This is the way walk in it'"* (Isaiah 30:21). This is God's promise to you. As you call out to Him...*Lord, please show me what I need to do next*...quiet yourself and allow Him to speak to your heart. As we discussed in Chapter 4, write out those prayers in your prayer journal and record whatever counsel God may impress on your heart.

What does the Bible say about why we are to seek godly counsel? Consider these verses.

- "The way of a fool seems right to him, but a wise man listens to advice" (Proverbs 12:15).
- "Listen to advice and accept instruction, and in the end you will be wise" (Proverbs 19:20).
- "Your Word is a lamp to my feet and a light to my path" (Psalm 119:105).

If you were to take out a highlighter right now to mark keywords, you begin to see the thread that connects these verses. A fool is someone who limits his or her counsel to his own thoughts of what is right. A wise man listens and accepts counsel from outside *sources*. I picture God's Word literally as being a lamp that illuminates the path in front of me, enabling me to safely take my next step. I like to picture "a light to my path" as being His floodlight for the roads further ahead.

God is teaching me to trust Him when I cannot see where I am going (which is often). When I choose to walk by faith (not by seeing), I walk in His light even when I cannot see. Precious child of God, do not allow the darkness of your situation to overcome you. You hold His perfect light when you hold onto His Word.

SEEK OUTSIDE COUNSEL

Godly counsel also includes seeking advice, opinions, and instructions for your situation from other people. Choose very wisely. Ask the Lord to lead you to someone safe and qualified that you may share with. Calling Focus on the Family for a counselor in your area might be a start. If your spouse is willing to go to marriage counseling with you, it can be a wonderful place for the two of you to learn how to improve your communication, talking to and listening to each other. Even a "bad" experience with a counselor, one where you both know that you don't want to go back to "that" one, can serve as a means of drawing you closer together. Our first counselor talked about himself most of the hour. It gave me and my husband something to agree on when we went to dinner together after our first session.

When I learned that there had been a serious breach of trust in my marriage, I reached out to a close friend who lives out of town. I knew I could trust her to pray for me and to keep what I shared confidential. I shared with no one else for the first six months. No one, that is, besides sharing with my Lord, my Abba Daddy. God knew how I was hurting, even before I poured my heart out to Him on the pages of my journal.

As my situation became more difficult, I sought additional counsel by calling Nancy, a woman in my church who had headed up the Women to Women mentoring program I had been involved in the year earlier. I had great respect for her walk with Jesus and felt like she was someone I could connect with. As I shared with her more of the details of my situation (the "sharing" felt more like I vomited them out on her), she had the experience and wisdom to know that I needed more than just a listening ear and her words of godly wisdom. She was gracious to continue to meet and talk one-on-one with me (and send me incredible words of encouragement via calls and texts), but she also gave me the name of a Christian counselor she knew well. She encouraged me to make an appointment with Stephanie who is a licensed Christian counselor.

GO AHEAD AND MAKE THE CALL

May I just say that making a call like that to a complete stranger is a very hard thing to do? What was I going to say when I called to schedule my appointment? I have to laugh at myself now as I think back on that day when her office returned the voicemail I'd left them earlier that morning. I somehow missed the part where the caller said she was calling *for Stephanie* and wasn't actually the counselor. Again, I "vomited" out much of my mess in random incoherent sentences onto the poor receptionist!

When we did get to meet (during our first session), Stephanie prayed aloud and asked God to reveal to me what He wanted me to know. In a moment of silence after our time of prayer, this is what God spoke to my heart: *Kirby, it is okay for you to be weak right now. Be a learner and not a teacher during this season. Be still and know that I am God.* I wept when I realized that He was giving me permission to be weak. All of us are weak at times. I desperately needed to hear these words of wisdom.

> **It is okay for you to be weak right now.**

In your weakness, allow a counselor to help you become strong, learning to grow into all that God has created you to be. Before you meet together, wherever you choose to go for help, ask the Lord to speak His wisdom into this person, so he or she can be an instrument for your healing. Beseech the Lord to enable you be wise in hearing and receiving the counsel you receive. You deserve that investment in yourself.

Chapter 8

IS FORGIVING MY ONLY OPTION? (IT'S A COMMAND, NOT A SUGGESTION)

The command in Scripture for us to forgive those who have sinned against us is a very big deal to God. If it is our aim to walk in obedience to God, then we must see His instruction to "forgive" as the command it is, rather than a mere suggestion. This point is made clear in "The Parable of the Unmerciful Servant" (Matthew 18:2-35) when Jesus answers Peter's question, *"Lord, how many times shall I forgive my brother when he sins against me? Up to seven times?"* What is Jesus' response? *"Not seven times, but seventy-seven times"* (basically, a limitless amount).

He goes on to describe a servant who begs his master to forgive him of a debt he owes the master. *"The servant's master took pity on him, canceled the debt and let him go."* This servant turns right around and finds a fellow servant who owes him a far smaller debt than the one his master had just forgiven him. As his fellow servant begs for patience in order to be able to pay off his debt, the recently forgiven (yet very ungrateful) man refuses to forgive the debt. Instead, he sends his fellow servant off to prison. When the first servant's master learns what has happened, he calls the ungrateful servant "wicked" and sends him to jail to be tortured until he can pay back all he owes. Jesus brings this message home to us when he says, *"This is how my heavenly Father will treat each of you unless you forgive your brother from your heart."*

The one who will not forgive always suffers more than the one who is not forgiven. Unforgiveness tortures the soul.

The one who will not forgive always suffers more....

THE COST OF CHOOSING NOT TO FORGIVE

If you are thinking that holding onto bitterness and unforgiveness is the one thing, by golly, you *don't* have to do because "he certainly doesn't deserve any more grace and forgiveness for the things he's done." Then please reread Matthew 18:34-35, as Jesus warns His disciple of the cost of choosing NOT to forgive: *"In anger his master turned him over to the jailers to be tortured...this is how my heavenly Father will treat each of you unless you forgive your brother from your heart."* Our jailer is Satan the deceiver, who delights in chaining us to the pains of our past. He wants more than to destroy our marriage. He wants to do everything he can to hinder us from experiencing any of the good God has for us. And if we let him, he will do so by seeing to it that our thoughts stay filled with resentments and negative images of our hurtful past.

When we refuse to allow our hearts to forgive the one who has caused us pain, the enemy tortures us by keeping us in a mind-set of being a victim of our circumstances. He robs us of the joy and peace and rest that we can have when we acknowledge the sovereignty of God and God's goodness. Satan wants each one of us to walk through the fire, and feel as though any life left in us has been burned up and consumed. He thrills when he is able to keep us from praising the Lord when we've been burned. The apostle John says, *"But whoever hates his brother is in the darkness and walks around in the darkness; he does not know where he is going, because the darkness has blinded him"* (1 John 2:11). To not forgive is to hate and to be blinded by the dark. Strong words to consider.

Please don't read further, thinking that you're not yet ready to forgive. Don't think you just "don't have it in you" to do this. Don't blow past this powerful Scripture, believing that Jesus' warnings of imprisonment and torture couldn't possibly apply to you because you weren't at fault in your situation. Or because your spouse never said he was sorry, never asked for forgiveness, or continues to hurt you after you forgave the last time. This isn't about "him."

FORGIVENESS - GOD'S GIFT TO YOU

Forgiveness is God's precious gift to YOU. Christ forgiving me of my own sins, and allowing Himself to be crucified on a cross because of my sins, is the greatest gift I have ever been given. So when He asks me to do the same, and He commands me (because He loves me so much and wants His best for me) to follow His example and forgive others, how can I not forgive?

Actually, I know, that humanly speaking, I can't. And honestly, nothing inside of me even wants to. But *"I know that I can do all things through Christ who gives me strength"* (Philippians 4:13). I know that God, if I ask Him, will give me the "want to" I need to forgive. And the indwelling of His Spirit within me will enable me to forgive when I *decide* to forgive.

Experiencing the *emotions* of walking in freedom as someone who is no longer haunted by past memories (because I have chosen to forgive) may take a long time. Because my wounds are deep. And I am still in stormy waters. Emotional forgiveness is a *process* which, with God's help, will happen with time. But the *decision* to forgive the one who has pained me can be done today. This is a decision that each one of us can make…NOW. We are to follow the apostle Paul's lead in saying, *"I forgive whatever needs to be forgiven...so that Satan will not outsmart us. For we are familiar with his evil schemes"* (2 Corinthians 2:10-11 NLT).

But what are we actually doing if we choose to forgive? Do we really know what forgiveness is? According to Dr. Dick Tibbits' excellent book, *Forgive to Live,* "forgiveness is the process of reframing one's anger and hurt from the past, with the goal of recovering one's peace and revitalizing one's purpose and hope for the future." He says that forgiveness defines who *you* are—it doesn't say that the other's wrongful act is right. Forgiveness is giving up your right to hurt or punish the one who hurt you. It frees you from the desire for vengeance and retaliation. It remains unhindered by the other person's actions or attitude in your decision to forgive. Their actions will now have less power to control you.

WHAT FORGIVENESS DOESN'T MEAN

Forgiveness does not necessarily lead to reconciliation. That process takes two. Forgiveness only takes one. Forgiveness doesn't mean we forget and our past memories are wiped clean. It doesn't mean that we excuse or condone the offensive act committed against us. In fact, forgiveness says that we are NOT okay with it, but that we are choosing to no longer hold the offense against the offender. Forgiveness does not mean that there aren't consequences for the sinful behavior. There will be. It does mean that your past won't keep offending and haunting you when you do remember. The past loses its hold on you so that healing can begin.

Let's say that the decision to forgive is made, and we have chosen to express our thankfulness to God for His forgiveness to us by following His command to forgive. How do we do it well? Start by allowing your every thought and feeling to be made captive to Christ. Begin by praying, *Lord, Your will. Your way.* Forgiveness will begin on the inside, but it's stronger if it can be visibly expressed on the outside as an act of love to your offender. This verbal expression of forgiveness for every act of betrayal is not always appropriate or best. Yet, when possible, showing your offender some kindness through a smile, a thank you for things done well, or a written letter of forgiveness, is an opportunity to be a reflection of Christ.

Dr. Tibbits says it so beautifully, that "our one little act of gracious generosity may be the nudge that shakes them loose from the bondage of regret, shame, and embarrassment." Our forgiveness then becomes a win for everyone, except for Satan! I have borrowed much in writing this chapter from the things I learned while reading, *Forgive to Live*. I discovered that, until now, I never really understood how crucial this word "forgiveness" actually is. Until I walked through this fire of mine, I had never before learned the lesson of true forgiveness.

DROP YOUR ROCKS

There is a parable called "Drop the Rock," which Tibbits includes in his writing, and I'd like to end this chapter by passing it along to you. The story begins when a powerful spell is cast on a town, that whenever an unkind or hurtful word is spoken, it instantly becomes a hot rock. Some people, when pelted by the rocks, chose to hold onto those rocks. Even though they caused them painful blisters on their hands. They held onto one or two in case they could use them to retaliate one day. They believed that the pain would be worth it. As the rocks began to cool the people would take their rocks to the center of the town where a pile accumulated. Rehashing old grievances with others in the town would cause the rocks to heat back up, reigniting the person's desire to throw a rock and cause some hurt again.

One day, "a cheerful man with compassion in his eyes" came into town and let them know they could be free of their heavy load of carrying rocks, and not have to live in misery any more. He said, "simply put, forgiveness is learning how to drop your rocks.

You don't have to collect them, carry them, be burdened by them, heat them, or throw them...your whole life will improve." It is time for us to drop our rocks of resentment. It is time to forgive the one who has hurt you. And if there is something within yourself which you are ashamed of, it is time to drop those rocks and forgive yourself as well.

I will end this chapter with a prayer that came to me from a friend: *Lord, I choose as an act of my will, to forgive my husband of all the things he has done to me, our family, and anyone else. In Jesus' mighty name! I also choose to bless him as I forgive him, and I put him in your hands.* Amen.

Chapter 9

CRANK UP THE PRAISE MUSIC!

I have struggled for days to get this chapter written. I've researched a lot of Scripture that pertains to praising the Lord, read from other sources, and asked for input from many friends. How do you write about something you can't fully grasp yourself? I think that I am finally beginning to understand that there is so much more to "keeping the praise music playing" than turning on my radio.

GOD INHABITS THE PRAISE OF HIS PEOPLE

Praising God is an attitude of the heart that finds joy when expressed through music. Unfortunately in the past, I have limited my efforts of praising God mostly to Sunday morning singing and singing aloud to Christian music in my car. "God inhabits the praise of His people" is an expression I have said many times but didn't know where in Scripture that phrase was found. My son Tucker led me to the old KJV which says it this way in Psalm 22:3. *"But thou art holy, O thou that inhabitest the praises of Israel."* Or God is *"enthroned on the praises of Israel"* (NLT). The Lord is near when we praise Him. Our praise and worship invites His presence in.

When we praise God, we come toward Him and He comes near to us in response. And look what takes place when Jesus meets with someone who is weary and distressed: *"Come to me all who are weak and weary and I will give you rest. Take My yoke upon you and learn from me, for I am gentle and humble in heart, and you will find rest for your souls. For my yoke is easy and my burden is light"* (Matthew 11:28-30). We find rest as He begins to replace our burdens with Christ himself.

PRAISE YOKES YOU WITH JESUS

To understand "yoke," picture two oxen joined by a single wooden double harness. The yoke harnesses the two animals closely side by side, as they plow through hard rocky places, pulling their heavy load behind. Our load is light because we are yoked with Jesus. He carries our worries and our load upon Himself. When we pray and when we praise, our hearts and minds are yoked closely together with our Lord. Our burdens become His and they are light. Because He is able. So why not praise Him?

Isaiah 41:30-31 paints an even grander picture of what it can look like when we call upon the Lord and allow Him to carry our burden. Putting our trust in God while walking on the hard and difficult paths allows us to stand tall and rise above our circumstances. *"Even youths grow tired and weary, and young men stumble and fall; but those who hope in the Lord will renew their strength. They will soar on wings like eagles; they will run and not grow weary, they will walk and not be faint."*

Does our "hope" have to be expressed in music and song? No, but what a powerful conduit through which our expression of hope can flow. I experienced this during the painful months following the birth of my son born with Down syndrome. Speaking words of hope or even receiving words of encouragement was not possible. My heart hurt too much. Yet one Sunday morning, when the praise music was playing, my depression began to lift and God's words of hope were able to enter. My eyes filled with tears that morning as my mouth filled with praise.

PRAISE ALLOWS YOU TO SOAR

The key to enduring hardships is to wrap ourselves so tightly around God in our praise that we end up soaring when He soars as we lift our voices up with songs of hope. His Spirit will ascends as high as His praise. He created His children for the purpose of glorifying Him and enjoying Him forever (Westminster Shorter Catechism). He certainly doesn't need our help for anything else. So why not get the praise music playing?

Throughout Scripture, God instructs His people to praise Him as they go out into battle. We see this in 2 Chronicles, when Judah was completely in despair because of being invaded. Their leader, Jehoshaphat was experiencing great fear. Jehoshaphat told his people to believe in God, and he assigned singers to praise Jehovah God. *"As they began to sing and praise, the Lord set ambushments against the men of Ammon and Moab and Mount Seir who were invading Judah, and they were defeated"* (2 Chronicles 20:22). At the very moment the praising began, the Lord started to respond— and they saw victory. God moves quickly in response to our praise.

Watchman Nee was a Christian college student in China in the 1920's. In his book, *The Finest of the Wheat,* he explains what happens when God's children are praising. Satan must flee! Nee writes, "Prayer frequently is a battle, but praise is victory. Prayer is spiritual warfare; praise is triumph. For this reason praise is what Satan hates most." He says that when we pray, we are still in our circumstance; but when we praise, we have risen above the circumstance. He encourages his readers to learn to praise God while the burden is still heavy, rather than waiting until the crisis has passed. When you feel overwhelmed and don't know what you should do, learn to praise Him.

> **"... praise is what Satan hates most."**

A great example of this is found in Acts 16:25-26 when Paul and Silas had been stripped and beaten and thrown into prison. *"Around midnight Paul and Silas were praying and singing hymns to God, and the other prisoners were listening to them. Suddenly, there was such a violent earthquake that the foundations of the prison were shaken. At once all the prison doors flew open, and everybody's chains came loose."* And not only that, their prison guard was so impressed with what he saw that he asked the two, *"Sirs, what must I do to be saved?"* So why not praise Him?

THE SACRIFICE OF PRAISE IS YOUR OFFERING

To praise God is to express a feeling of admiration and gratitude to Him. Praise shows respect and reverence to the One we look to as King. Praise is us making much of who God is by magnifying, applauding, and lifting up His attributes. Praising God takes the focus off of ourselves and our own mess, and focuses our hearts on the One who is perfect and good. God showed His people in the Old Testament how they were to worship Him through this elaborate design of the tabernacle, or Tent of Meeting, described in Exodus 40. By means of this earthly tabernacle, God came to dwell or "tabernacle" with His people. He took up residence there. In order for someone to properly worship this perfect God, He required an unblemished male animal to be sacrificed on the brazen altar as a payment for their sins against God.

Two thousand years ago, in the beginning of the New Testament, Jesus Christ paid the requirement for that blood sacrifice on our behalf, once and for all. He did this when He gave up his own blameless life on the cross. Fortunately, we no longer need to secure a thrashing animal on an altar in order to come in and enjoy God's presence. Surrendering our lives to the lordship of Christ is what God asks of us. Christ's sacrifice provides access for me to come close to God.

I am ushered into the presence of the living God when I can raise my hands in adoration to the God who loves me. I'm drawn close to Him when I sing His praises, especially when walking through the fires of life. I don't think there is a sweeter sound to our Father's ears than to hear His children pouring out their faith through praise. And it is all the sweeter when those praises flow from a heart that's been wounded. This is our sacrifice of praise that is pleasing and acceptable to God. And our victory comes when His Spirit begins to work in our heart, healing our hurt. Victory begins when He lifts us up out of our suffering through praise, even if for a moment.

PRAISE BEING PUT TO THE TEST

In between the writing of these pages, I've had the opportunity to put "Praising God" to the test. Some really upsetting words were spewed upon me just before someone was walking out the back door. The words caught me by surprise. The comments were hurtful and the hours that followed could've been a downer, if I had let my attention stay focused on the venomous vapors that were left swirling in the air. INSTEAD, I began to sing God's praises. No radio, I just sang from my heart. *And the chains that were trying to fasten themselves around me crashed to the ground and were gone.* Hallelujah. The enemy has no power in my praise! *Lord, I sing praises to Your name. Because You alone are worthy of all praise, and because I know that You inhabit the praise of Your people.*

"The trumpeters and singers joined in unison, as with one voice, to give praise and thanks to the Lord...they raised their voices in praise to the Lord and sang: 'He is good; his love endures forever.' Then, the temple of the Lord was filled with a cloud...for the glory of the Lord filled the temple of God" (2 Chronicles 5:13). Why not keep the praise music playing and praise Him?

Chapter 10

WATCH YOUR MOUTH -
IT CAN BITE YOU
(JUST BECAUSE YOU HAVE THE AMMO,
YOU DON'T HAVE TO SHOOT)

The temptation to "let 'em have it" with my words or to "give him an earful" of the sarcastic responses which sit in the roof of my mouth is palpable. My flesh fights to lash out with hurtful comments. I've got a lot of ammunition from which to fire. Words that when spoken, would not be spoken with grace and certainly not with the Father's blessings. They would wound and anger the one they are spoken about.

Yet would these words feel good coming out? I wish I wasn't able to answer that question from personal experience. But I can. And yes, sometimes they feel really good coming out. But they don't *leave* me feeling good and clean and at peace within. The pleasure is extremely short lived, and not worth the consequence.

When I'm able to hold these angry wounding words back, I sense that I am not the one who is restraining them. The Holy Spirit is doing a work in me. He is taking away my desire to hurt others with my words. His Spirit enables God's grace to flow *through* me as I speak. And I am grateful for that. I could unleash a barrage full of destructive sarcasm. However, I know that *"Do not let any unwholesome talk come out of your mouth"* from Ephesians 4:29 is not a suggestion. It is a command given to each one of us by God. The Lord is also teaching me to silence others' argumentative comments and offenses with a *humble* response. I pray, *Oh God, that my mouth would not sin. Holy Spirit, hold me accountable.* And God then helps me to guard my lips.

THE ENEMY WANTS YOUR HARSH WORDS TO HURT YOU

So why does God find it so important that we guard our tongue from harsh words? Why does He then ask us to go even a step further? To build others up? When I have felt beaten down by others, is "building someone up" what I feel like doing? Absolutely not.

> But speaking "unwholesomeness" opens a window to our soul for the enemy to do his number on us.

Harsh words are of benefit to no one except *"the thief who comes only to steal and kill and destroy"* (John 10:10). The enemy will see to it that your brief momentary feelings of vindication in lashing out with your tongue will start eating at you. Don't go there. Instead, take your feelings to the Father in prayer.,

Lord, take away the seeds of resentment and bitterness in me. In the name of Jesus—leave! Resentment, you are not welcome here. I am blessed beyond measure. There is no room in me for unrighteous anger or malice or resentment or any bitterness whatsoever. Lord, fill me instead with Your grace that abounds. Amen.

Guard your tongue so that you will guard your heart. Me speaking harshly and with no restraint only adds drama to the drama. If my intent is to cause others to think less about the one I am speaking of, even if what I am speaking is the truth...it is slander. And slander is listed in Scripture right in there with *"rage and anger, brawling...and every form of malice"* (Ephesians 4:31). God tells us to GET RID OF such things. Jesus said to the crowd in Matthew 15:10-11, *"Listen and understand. What goes into a man's mouth does not make him 'unclean,' but what comes out of his mouth, that is what makes a man unclean."*

ROTTEN TALK SPREADS ROTTENNESS

Are you clear on what "unwholesome talk" includes? Other Bible translations of this verse call it foul or abusive language. They refer to unwholesome talk as corrupt communication. Hateful words. Filthy talk. Foul or corrupt means "rotten." And rotten spreads more rottenness to everyone who hears. The simplest litmus test to consider before speaking a word is asking yourself this. Might speaking my words hurt another person? Ouch!

Instead of unwholesome talk, we are to let everything we say be helpful for building others up. According to *their* needs. That it may BENEFIT those who listen. Our words are to be good and helpful. They are to be an encouragement to those who hear them. They are to give grace to our listeners and be edifying to other people's needs. If I speak with words and a tone of voice which bring honor to the Lord, then those people who hear my words will be less likely to respond with negative and destructive words. Even if they may be thinking them. If I remain firm in choosing words which bless rather than curse, then I set a precedent for how a conversation is likely to go.

Look back further at Ephesians 4:26-27 (NLT): *"And don't sin by letting anger control you. Don't let the sun go down while you are still angry, for anger gives a foothold for the devil."* Scripture teaches us that feeling angry is not a sin. Rather it is how we allow that anger to *express* itself that leads to sin. As much as what we speak is to be a benefit to *others* who listen, the command to guard our lips is also for our *own* good and protection.

I see evidence that God is at work inside of me when the Holy Spirit enables me to do something I am unable to do. Which is to choose to build others up and bless them with my words even when their words have hurt me. As a result, what others experience is *"the fragrance of the knowledge God"* and the sweet *"aroma of Christ"* (2 Corinthians 2:14-15). God gives us a beautiful opportunity in this to experience real joy. When we reflect Christ in our conversations with others, they get to experience the presence and power of God for themselves. Watching this happen is where you will find your joy!

SPEAK BLESSINGS INSTEAD

Clearly, our speech is of utmost importance to the Father. Trust Him on this. Just as your choice to *forgive* the one who has hurt you is for your good, so also your choice to *speak blessings* instead of curses is for your own good. It is an act of obedience to God's Word. Both forgiveness and speaking blessings mean that you are giving up your right to punish the one who hurt you. Even though the pain and possible scars you have suffered may be with you for a long time. The great gift for me is that each time I choose to obey in these two areas, the hurts and the wounds fade.

Consider these words before you speak: *"Let your conversation be always full of grace, seasoned with salt, so that you may know how to answer everyone"* (Colossians 4:6). Consider this prayer before you respond: *"Set a guard over my mouth, O Lord; Keep watch over the door of my lips. Let not my heart be drawn to what is evil"* (Psalm 141:3). What a wonderful prayer to pray before answering a phone call from an old friend who's just heard "some news" and wants to hear more from you. Be prayed up and prepared to have your conversation with that friend. Remember, your story is not over. Don't ruin it with your mouth.

Chapter 11

GO AHEAD AND CRY:
IT'S A GRIEVING PROCESS

Twila Paris wrote a song I listened to years ago called, "The Warrior is a Child." The song was about a person who, to others, appeared to be a strong and amazing warrior on the outside. In actuality, this person on the inside was but a frightened child who was holding back tears and desperate for a good cry. I used to stand in my kitchen and belt out the words of the chorus. My husband's job training had taken our family far away from everything and everyone familiar to us. I was incredibly lonely. It somehow felt very therapeutic to sing and to cry at the same time.

This song reminds me that sometimes I just need to be still and allow God to fight my battles. We cannot stay strong all the time. I've been singing that song a lot lately, and today has been one of those days. I'm going through the motions with the tasks I have committed to. Pushing myself to do the next thing. Yet I feel no joy inside me right now, no reason to smile. I've learned to "push" the outer corners of my mouth in an

> **Sometimes I just need to be still and allow God to fight my battles.**

upward direction when I stand in front of other people, in order to hide the sadness I'm feeling on the inside.

Today, I don't feel like trying to be strong. I'd really rather crawl back in bed and pull the covers way up over my head and sleep for a long, long time. I'm so grateful my Abba Daddy picks this wounded child up when I don't feel up to doing battle. He rocks me gently and lovingly in His arms. Romans 8:26 says even when we don't know what to pray for, *"the Holy Spirit intercedes for the saints (that's us believers) with groans that words cannot express" (parentheses mine).* How incredibly comforting to know that He hears our cries and intercedes to Jesus on our behalf. We don't even have to know what to pray.

FEELINGS OF SADNESS COME UNANNOUNCED

Allow yourself a good cry. Several cries are fine, too. When I seem to be doing pretty well, keeping my focus on all that I have to be grateful for and how faithful the Lord has been thus far, feelings of sadness will hit me unannounced. *"My soul is downcast within me"* (Psalm 42:6). The gravity of it all seeps in. I'm alone, and this is permanent. Why were we not worth fighting for?

I hate using this word, but I just have to say it like it is. This *sucks.* There it is. Not very spiritual sounding, and I don't think I've ever seen it in Scripture. Though I think King David may have been tempted to use it while hiding out in a cave, afraid for his life. Or maybe Joseph, who felt forgotten while in prison. Sometimes the word just fits.

DEAR LORD, HEAR MY CRY

I'm just low and sad and down, yet I have no desire to wallow here for long. Hear my cry, Lord. For comfort, for security, for Your help.

And He answers me...

Kirby, go to My Word. Cast your burdens on Me, and I will wash them away and carry you. Do not worry or be afraid. This is not a surprise to Me. This process, precious daughter, is part of My Plan and I am working it all out for your good. Remember that "good" is conforming you and others closer and closer into the image of Christ. Cling to Me. Keep your eyes fixed on Jesus, and your disappointments will fall away. Despair cannot have a grip on you when your eyes stay fixed on Me and my glory.

GET THE HELP YOU NEED

When we recognize and can admit that we are sad, we hopefully can then extend ourselves a little extra grace for the moment (and an extra scoop of frozen chocolate yogurt to sweeten the sadness). But a good cry need not go on and on. If you are finding yourself doing this each day for more than a couple weeks, I would strongly encourage you to talk with your physician to see if you may benefit from some additional help. Personally, I am grateful that a little pill can raise my "feel good" serotonin level and help me feel like me. There is no shame in needing medical help. It is certainly not for everybody, but it can be very beneficial for those who need it. God has equipped many good physicians and healthcare workers to meet the needs of His precious children. He wants us to get the help we need, all the while keeping our eyes fixed on Him.

Whenever I let my eyes drift off of Jesus, I get sucked right up into the storm. And for a moment, I feel like a boat without its rudder or its sail. A boat that can catch no wind and is unable to stay on course. Just out there in the water, going nowhere.

Yet how am I supposed to know where this boat is sailing? The boat I was on for all those years of my marriage was heading toward an empty nest. Toward retirement. Trips to new places. Together. I really didn't have to know where the boat was going. My husband knew, and I was along for the ride as his shipmate. And some of that ride was happy sailing. Some of it was not. This has left me needing to learn how to navigate a new vessel on a different course. This has left me needing to catch the wind back in my sails. And somehow, it has left me at peace.

My boat is indeed more peaceful. Yet at times I am still sad. Sad and overwhelmed because this is so hard. My world has been rocked. My identity changed. So much information coming into my head from counseling, books, and videos. Often I can't quiet my mind. I am emotionally exhausted—spent—done.

I have never before tried to learn how to set up a new email account. To open my own bank account. To figure out retirement investments. I rarely planned out my own weekends because I was a "we" and he did the planning. He did all of that. It probably wasn't something he liked to do either. But he did. He took care of a whole lot of stuff that I know very little about.

I WAS A "WE" WHO HAD LOST MUCH OF "ME"

Now at 57, my brain is being asked to wake up and start moving. Honestly, I didn't know if I was capable of learning new tasks. Much of my brain felt dormant and out to pasture. I have dedicated myself to being a mom and a homemaker (not that those two great tasks put one's brain in retirement!). I have no regrets whatsoever for my decision to put my focus on my family, but in the process, a big part of me died. I've been saying that to myself for the past two years. In retrospect, I am seeing that the death of me came as I poured so much of my energy and focus into being a keeper of the peace, which I'll address in the next chapter. Maybe some of my grieving is realizing how much of "me" I have lost over the years.

My precious counselor, Stephanie, who has been such a source of strength to me, reminded me that much of the tears and sadness come to us because we are grieving. We are grieving the loss of a dream. And grieving is a process, a necessary process we must work through by admitting there has been a real loss. Drawing from Elisabeth Elliot's words in *Be Still My Soul*, we see that acceptance of our circumstances (including this place you are in *right now*) is the response God desires: "Peace and joy and faith will not be found in forgetting, and they will not be found in busyness or aloofness or the submission of defeat. They will not be found in anger at the 'unfairness' of it all."

SUFFERING CAN BE A CATALYST FOR NEEDED CHANGE

One of the beautiful gifts of our suffering is that it often makes us desperate to hear from God—desperate to make sense of the betrayal, or at least to find hope for the days to come. No one likes to suffer. For those of us who have worked hard at avoiding conflict in a relationship (a symptom of being a peacekeeper), experiencing the pain of emotional suffering may be the catalyst we need for change. And that is a good thing.

I've heard it said that "insanity" can be defined as someone repeating the same behavior over and over yet expecting a different result. Not smart, but when someone is worn down emotionally, it is easy to fall into some pretty insane patterns in a relationship. Yet the "status quo" is not acceptable if the relationship itself causes you to suffer or even "settle" for less than you believe is good. I accepted an unhealthy "status quo," yet Jesus came for so much more than to have us merely exist. He came that we might experience *abundant* life. If your heart is crying out, wanting more than you are experiencing now, this isn't a selfish yearning. God puts inside of us this desire for more of Him, a desire for more closeness with the One you love, a desire for a more abundant life.

God is such a generous and gracious Father that He wants the best for His sons and daughters. He wants His children to experience fruitful living, rich in love, joy, peace, patience, kindness, and goodness. My own marriage didn't just suddenly turn from dreamy-divine to broken. I cried out to the Lord for years, *God, I want more, more in my marriage!* I cannot go back and change the past, yet I wonder how much of the past seasons of suffering in my marriage could have served as catalysts for me to seek counsel and change.

WE ARE NOT CONSUMED

Jesus came to give us life in abundance. *"Because of the Lord's great love we are not consumed (destroyed), for his compassions never fail. They are new every morning; great is your faithfulness. I say to myself, 'The Lord is my portion; Therefore I will wait on him, to the one who seeks me.' The Lord is good to those whose hope is in him, to the one who seeks him"* (parentheses mine) (Lamentations 3:22-25). How absolutely applicable is this verse? I have felt consumed and all used up for a long time. That would give any of us reason for a good cry, don't you think?

Part of me wants to wallow in this being a "victim" mode. Saying, "Look what I've been through!" But this leaves me feeling tarnished and sad. Lean into this: *We are not consumed because the Lord loves us greatly. He loves YOU greatly! "His compassions never fail"* (Lamentations 3:22). Compassion literally means to "suffer together" (*Greater God Magazine*).

If the God of the Universe, the Sovereign Creator is suffering together with me, if He is collecting my tears, and if His Word promises I will not be consumed, then I have reason to celebrate! He is my faithful prince, and I will wait on Him to get me through all of this. *"And God will wipe every tear from their eyes"* (Revelations 7:17). He will not allow a single tear of yours to go without notice.

Chapter 12

ARE YOU A PEACEMAKER
OR A PEACEKEEPER?

"*Keep the peace* in your home whatever the cost." Is that what God's Word tells us to do? I only recently realized how WRONG and enabling my idea of peacekeeping actually is. It isn't healthy.

It also isn't fair to others that I just assume they know how I really feel about an issue, when I don't verbalize my feelings. It isn't fair that I'm overly sensitive to other people's remarks if I haven't spoken up to say, "That hurt me." It isn't fair to others that I assume a certain look I give, sigh I breathe, or hand on my hip has a clear meaning as to what I'm thinking. I didn't understand there is a major difference between being a peacekeeper and being a peacemaker.

In Jesus' teachings to His disciples in the Sermon on the Mount, also known as the Beatitudes, He says this. *"Blessed are the peace-MAKERS, for they will be called sons of God"* (Matthew 5:9). Here is what I am learning as I study this passage. According to Warren Wiersbe's Bible commentary, the word "blessed" describes an "inner satisfaction and sufficiency that does not depend on outward circumstances for happiness [emphasis mine]." Blessed is a divine joy. It's a God thing. A peacemaker is someone who tries to *cause* peace to happen. Its definition includes helping others solve conflict and reach a peaceful solution. This doesn't sound like too many of the conversations my spouse and I have had in recent years. A synonym for peacemaker is "reconciler." PeaceMAKING would have us collaborating together to make decisions so that both of us get something we want or need. Talking it out together to create solutions where we can both find peace. Blessed are the peacemakers.

SO WHAT'S THE DIFFERENCE?

Now look at some of the definitions of peacekeeper, the word I inaccurately believed for years was a picture of biblical submission. The peacekeeper is a person who maintains or restores peace and amity. She is someone who tries to keep things peaceful often by calming people down. I now see that what I was doing was similar to holding a lid on a boiling pot. Probably two boiling pots. His and mine. What I was doing was swallowing hard the words I needed to express because I wasn't up for the conflict I knew those words would stir. And each time I swallowed instead of expressing what I needed to say, I lost a part of my voice. I lost myself.

> **Each time I swallowed instead of expressing what I needed to say, I lost a part of my voice.**

Peacekeeper is *not* the word Jesus chose to use to bless us with His divine joy. It's not even listed in my Bible concordance! Keeping the peace may allow two people to get through a tense moment with civility and without *outward* fighting. But the tension and turmoil only builds within, like steam building in a boiling pot. This is where resentments begin to fester. This is feeding ground for the enemy. I now know that God wants so much more for His children.

Consider this prayer as you seek to become a better peacemaker: *Change me Jesus. Change the condemning look in my eyes when I feel hurt. Instead, teach me to speak with love and clarity about what I need. Teach me to express my hurt in a way that honors You. Help my new way of expressing my hurts to draw me and my offender closer together because of it. Give me your voice, Lord, to speak up for truth and for goodness and kindness. I don't want to lose my voice, my passion for the things that matter. Teach me to confront words that are spoken in anger. Help me to confront them with love and gentleness and grace, so they will lose their power. Amen.*

Chapter 13

BE SHREWD AS A SERPENT
AND INNOCENT AS A DOVE

Seeking legal counsel is never the place in which a person wants to find themselves in the context of marriage. For me, after learning that trust had severely been broken in my marriage, the mere thought of considering whether or not to consult an attorney felt like giving up on 35 years of marriage. It felt as if I was somehow betraying my husband by doing something in secret. The fear of him finding out I had consulted an attorney competed with a greater fear of what could happen to me if things continued the way they were going. I had not ever envisioned being in such a place before, and I certainly didn't want to be at this place of talking with a lawyer.

AM I BEING SELFISH OR WISELY CONCERNED?

Fortunately, I have found peace in learning that God, in His Word, has addressed how believers are to behave when facing a challenging endeavor. As Christians, we are expected to represent Jesus Christ to others who are watching, even if (and especially if) we have been mistreated. Months ago as the circumstances in my marriage seemed to be spiraling out of control, I asked the Lord this: *God, please help. Am I seeing this wrong? Am I being selfish here or wisely concerned? Help me to cling tightly to You in these days when I am being left hanging. Please give me Your peace in the wait. Show me what to do.*" God led me directly to Matthew 10:16. *"I am sending you out like sheep among wolves. Therefore be as shrewd as snakes and as innocent as doves."* I was certain this was the verse He was showing me, but not so clear initially as to its meaning.

"Shrewd" isn't a word that has ever been in my vocabulary. I had to look up the word and do a lot of outside reading on serpents, doves, sheep, and wolves to grasp what Jesus meant in these instructions. Jesus was giving directions to His disciples as He sent them out to minister "to the wolves." The profound power of our Lord's words in this verse are mind blowing. Only through the equipping of Christ inside us can we possess the best of attributes from *both* a serpent and a dove. Although the evil, conniving actions of Satan are often attached to the serpent, Jesus would have us look to the positive attributes of this animal when asking us to be shrewd as a snake. Snakes are very sharp sighted, strong, intelligent, subtle, and shrewd. They tend to mind their own business rather than expose themselves to unnecessary danger, quickly retreating under rocks to avoid harm.

A person is shrewd or prudent when he or she is acting with care and thought for the future. She is shrewd when she becomes a keen listener. And she is shrewd when she acts wisely in her relationships with others. These are *desirable* assets to own. Jesus, just like the apostle Paul, showed shrewdness by possessing discernment to understand the different mindsets of the people He was speaking to. He showed shrewdness by speaking to each group according to what *they* needed to hear. For some, Jesus used parables, while with others He was straight up blunt. Both of His responses were being shrewd.

A dove, on the other hand, is seen as an animal that is

harmless, vulnerable, and innocent. Doves were considered clean animals and thus used for sacrifices in the Old Testament. A dove has always been a symbol of peace.

So what does this mean for those of us who have found ourselves in a mess and needing to seek protection? How are we to proceed?

STAND UP FOR YOURSELF - GOD'S WAY

Jesus, in Matthew 10:16 is suggesting that we combine the wisdom of the serpent with the harmlessness of a dove. The serpent's wisdom will spare us unnecessary exposure to danger, including financial danger, and the dove's harmlessness will spare us from taking a course of action that is selfish and sinful. John Gill, in his *Exposition of the Bible*, describes beautifully what our character should look like as we move forward in an effort to protect ourselves. Here are our guidelines to try and follow: *"Be free from all wicked cunning and craftiness...without malice and wrath, not meditating and seeking revenge, but meek and humble, leading inoffensive lives, and proceeding in the course of (our) calling."* We have a calling to stand up for what is right and fair. Yet we are called to do so without deceit or lying.

Allow God's Spirit to work within you to speak with tenderness to the one who has hurt you. Always tell the truth. *"You are to live clean, innocent lives as children of God in a dark world full of people who are crooked and stubborn. Shine out among them like beacon lights"* (Philippians 2:15 TLB). You can be innocent as a dove AND wise!

Meeting with an attorney does NOT mean divorce. It does mean that you are making an effort to educate yourself rather than keeping your head in the sand and remaining clueless. That sounds harsh, but there does come a time when you have to stand up for yourself and your children. Recognize that the enemy likely has been at work in your spouse, and the enemy will continue to try to distract and destroy *both* of you. There is no harm in becoming informed.

When I asked what advice my attorney has for someone dealing with a breach of trust in their marriage, he said this: "I would say referrals are the best way to find a good domestic attorney. You start with the people you know, love, and respect. Meet a few of these attorneys and educate yourself on the issues in your case and develop your goals. Even if the attorney is not for you, take advantage of the opportunity to educate yourself and fine tune your goals. Every case is different. The best attorney for you may not be the best attorney for your friend. Then do your due diligence...look at bios, internet reviews, bar info, etc. You are looking for the right combination of experience, morals/ethics, aggressiveness, and beliefs (not necessarily in that order)."

The first attorney I consulted was very informative and businesslike, but not a good fit for me. The attorney I chose, a recommendation from a trusted friend, has helped me to walk down this difficult path of legal matters in the manner I believe Jesus has instructed, shrewd as a serpent and innocent as a dove.

Chapter 14

COUNT YOUR BLESSINGS, LITERALLY

Count your blessings. Regularly and literally! Learn the art of giving thanks in all circumstances. This will cushion the blow of trials when they come against you. I am grateful for a book I read several years ago, *One Thousand Gifts: A Dare To Live Fully Right Where You Are*, by Ann Voskamp. She says that "gratitude [is] the preeminent attitude of the Christ-follower...the foremost quality of a believing disciple." She invites her reader to embrace a lifestyle of gratitude and to experience God in the moment. I have been following her suggestion since reading her book and am at over 3000 "Blessings," which I keep a running tab on in the back of whatever prayer journal I'm currently using. Some examples of the things I am grateful to God for: *Cool air outside this morning, birds singing, good check up with B's surgeon, hearing the kids laugh as they were sword fighting last night, sheer happiness after the volleyball game, being able to breathe through my nose (no Afrin!).* These are all reminders to me of how God provides in the big and small things.

This discipline of capturing my gratitude in an ongoing list has been great ammunition against the enemy, who prefers that

> **Capturing my gratitude in an ongoing list has been great ammunition against the enemy.**

I grumble and complain about the things that are not going my way. Some mornings it feels like a strain to come up with anything at all that I am thankful for because my focus is on the negative. Yet as I pause to reflect, I can easily add to my list of blessings just by starting at the top of my head: *No more sinus headaches, my hair stopped falling out, able to sleep well once I fell asleep last night.* If nothing comes to mind to write down, I ask God to open my eyes to those things I can thank Him for. And I wait on Him.

Philippians 2:14-15 tells us to *"do everything without complaining or arguing, so that you may become blameless and pure, children of God without fault in a crooked and depraved generation."* It breathes life into my day to speak thankfulness rather than grumbling (and it's a blessing to those around me as well). As followers of Christ we can always be grateful for whose we are in Christ. Grateful to be children of the King and co-heirs of Christ.

As Christians, we are forgiven and redeemed and loved unconditionally by our Heavenly Father. We can thank Him for our eternal home that awaits us and the realization that this life isn't "it." We are just passing through. And for those days when I am feeling completely overwhelmed by my life, I can thank God that heaven is looking sweeter and sweeter to me. You get the picture. Because He is a God of great mercy and hope, we are truly blessed.

Sarah Young, writer of *Jesus Calling*, reminds us of what happened to Eve in the beautiful Garden of Eden. Eve focused on the one fruit she could NOT have, rather than being thankful for all the good things she already had. Young writes that "the negative focus darkened her mind." The same can be true of us. In a later entry, Young beautifully states that "a thankful heart opens windows of heaven." Yes it does! So let's be like the psalmist and say, *"I will worship you and offer you a sacrifice of thanksgiving"* (Psalm 116:17). We can offer the Lord our tears and our praises.

Chapter 15

STEER CLEAR OF NEGATIVE
AND BITTER PEOPLE

Be very careful who you spend your time with. When your marriage takes a hit, and you find yourself in a confusing and difficult place, you are especially vulnerable to the opinions and well-meaning advice of others (or *not* so well-meaning, for that matter). With close to 1 out of every 2 marriages in America ending in divorce, there are plenty of folks around us who will have their own "marriage gone bad" stories to share and compare. I had no idea! Though it may feel momentarily "therapeutic" when we find someone to commiserate our woes with, we need to be on our guard.

DON'T LET THE ENEMY MESS WITH YOUR HEAD
If our goal is to follow God's lead through this rocky and challenging path and honor Him in the way we choose to walk it, and our desire is to keep the enemy from wreaking havoc in our heads and hearts, then we should limit the time we spend with negative and bitter people. In Chapter 9, we talked about being careful not to let unwholesome, unedifying talk come out of our own mouth.

The same principal holds true for what we allow ourselves to listen to from others. These negative people may be your neighbors, co-workers, or even close friends. Or they might be your own family members who have also felt hurt and betrayed because of what has happened to you (because the betrayal, in some ways, has now happened to *them*). Each person will have their own way of processing what has taken place. Their advice for you to seek revenge and slander may come out of a deep love and concern for you. However, that bitter seed planted inside you can still grow... regardless of who planted it.

May I just say, there are also folks out there who have no desire to keep their talk "wholesome"—they just like to gossip. And their "reaching out to you" is NOT with your best interests in mind! Guard yourself. Listening to the "scoop" about your man from people who are keeping you informed by what they've seen or heard, or the bad rap about someone else's man, has much the same effect on us as unforgiveness. It puts our focus on those things that are not *"true...noble...admirable...praiseworthy"* (Philippians 4:8) and it opens the door (or at least a window) for the enemy to come in and mess with us. Keep those doors and windows locked!

If knowing the details about your spouse's actions or words is not needed in order for you to make informed decisions on your future actions (i.e., determining if there is a legitimate need to separate or in regards to legal action), save yourself the trauma. Don't go there. *"Their tongues practice deceit. The poison of vipers is on their lips. Their mouths are full of cursing and bitterness. Their feet are swift to shed blood (or reputations); ruin and misery mark their ways and the way of peace they do not know. There is no fear (reverence) of God before their eyes"* (Romans 3:13). Ask God to give you the discernment to know when you are with these kinds of people. Ask Him to give you a "red flag" if a conversation is going south *before* it goes there!

> **Often, others will take your lead on how and where a conversation is to travel.**

When someone asks you, "Tell me what happened?" and you give a response such as, "There was a breach of trust in our marriage," your unwillingness to share details may deter further probing. Questions asked to you such as, "How are you holding up?" or "How can I pray for you?" or "What are your plans?" are a different type of probing. They are for your good. It is good to share our burdens, but without being destructive to other people. If your words in regards to your spouse are not biting and condemning, hopefully others will sense that you aren't interested in them "going there" either.

Corinthians 2:14-15 talks about believers spreading everywhere the *"fragrance of the knowledge of God,"* that we are the *"sweet aroma of Christ to those around us."* God's grace has never smelled sweeter to me than it has this year, in contrast to the "stink" and putrid mess I've been dragged into. As painful and difficult as this season of life has been for me, I've truly had some of the sweetest conversations with others about the goodness of God, ever. So if the atmosphere of the conversations you find yourself in "smells bad," do whatever you can to graciously get yourself out of it as quickly as possible.

ARE YOU TORMENTING YOURSELF?

With Facebook and social media at our fingertips, we have the ability to research (or have our friends research for us) all kinds of information to piece together what our spouse is up to, "just so we'll know." Why torment yourself? Consuming yourself with this kind of activity will serve no good purpose within your heart. Nada. Unfortunately for me, it always lingers in my head for several days after I hear "news" from someone who's seen my spouse, regardless of what he's been up to. The details can make my mind go into anxious overdrive, running down all kinds of unnecessary scenarios and roads which mentally, physically, and emotionally are capable of triggering anyone's demise. (As it happens, today is one of those days when I'm trying to figure out if I'm angry, sad, mad, or just still grieving.) Guard your ears. Guard your eyes. And as we talked about in Chapter 9, guard your tongue.

Remember God has *"plans to prosper you and not to harm you, plans to give you a hope and a future"* (Jeremiah 29:11). Sometimes that promise seems impossible. Yet in Christ, all things are possible. We are working to guard our hearts not only to *survive* our trials, but also to *receive* the abundant life which the Lord has promised to those who follow Him. Even though I'm not *feeling* life in abundance right now, I know that God is good. I know He has a good plan which He's working out for me in the midst of this mess. If I can avoid people who feed putting me into a critical, vindictive mood, I can help keep my state of mind in a better place. A critical mood leaves me with the harsh idea that I am somehow better than others. I am not. Except by the grace of God, I could be the one in our marriage who crossed the line.

Chapter 16

GO GET YOUR MANNA

In Old Testament times, when Moses was leading the Israelites out of Egypt to the Promise Land, their journey through the wilderness ended up taking them 40 long years to complete. Throughout their years in the desert, God was faithful to provide for all His people's needs. He made it so their clothing and sandals would never wear out. God provided food and water enough to sustain two million Israelites. He caused water to flow out from the rocks and He rained food down from heaven every morning. The Israelites would awaken to see the ground outside their tents covered with a wafer-like substance called manna. They would see the glory of the Lord in His faithful provision every day.

What is important to take note of here is that God made this "bread from heaven" available to His children, but He did not spoon feed it to them. The people had to ask themselves, "Am I going to lie here and stay hungry or am I going to get up and gather what God has provided for me?" They had to make a choice each day to GET UP AND GET OUT of their tents in order to receive God's provision. He taught

> **They had to make a choice each day to GET UP AND GET OUT of their tents...**

the Israelites to trust and rely on Him for their daily bread, one day at a time. And He wants to teach us to do the same.

God continues to be faithful to His children. Just like with the Israelites, God provides for our needs today. He uses those people around us to meet our needs. He uses the ministries in our churches, Bible studies, radio broadcasts, and even the internet to help us navigate waters we've never seen. If God has allowed the circumstances you find yourself in right now, then He will be faithful to equip you to walk through them. Because God is good.

But we MUST do our part. We have to choose to push those covers back each morning and get ourselves out of bed. We must choose to step out and partake of God's provision. And on those days we don't have the strength to "step out of our tents," we must humble ourselves and make a call to someone who can come alongside and help us get the help we need. This is the glory of God, revealed through the provision of His people.

Just like daily manna, the Lord's grace and mercies are new for us every morning. Though God is our Comforter, He desires to raise up His children to be strong. What has happened to you did NOT take God by surprise. It didn't catch Him off guard or make Him unable to respond to the needs you have today. " 'I know the plans I have for you,' declares the Lord. 'Plans to prosper you and not to harm you. Plans to give you a hope and a future' " (Jeremiah 29:11). What is our part today?

"Remember how the Lord your God led you all the way in the desert these forty years, to humble you and to test you in order to know what was in your heart, whether or not you would keep his commands. He humbled you, causing you to hunger and then feeding you with manna, which neither you nor your fathers had known, to teach you that man does not live on bread alone but on every word that comes from the mouth of the Lord" (Deuteronomy 8:2-3).

Chapter 17

TEMPTED TO DISCONNECT?
DARE TO SHARE

---

*Two are better than one, because they have a good return
for their work: If one falls down, his friend can help him
up. But pity the man who falls and has no one to help him
up! Though one may be overpowered, two can defend
themselves. A cord of three strands is not quickly broken.*
ECCLESIASTES 4:9-10,12

We were never ever called to go this road alone, not in the good
times, and certainly not in the bad times. God created us to be in
fellowship with Him and with one another. Two or three friends,
who share the same mindset of putting God at the head of all their
decisions, is far safer and stronger than you trying to stand alone.
Joined together in prayer and support, you can resist the enemy
who has come to bring you down through this fire. There is a Jew-
ish proverb that says a person without a friend is like a left hand
without a right. Not very productive. But with both hands together,
the saying goes, "much more can be accomplished and every

activity is easier." And I say "Amen" to that!

AVOID THE TEMPTATION TO DISCONNECT

The temptation to disconnect is palpable at times. Especially when we are in despair. There were (and still are, though much less often) days when I've felt so discouraged and low that I didn't want to bring someone else's day down with my problems. In the initial months of the marital bombshell, to protect my spouse, I confided in one friend only. I considered carrying the load alone but knew better. My head and heart would explode. I have had the privilege of walking through quite a few of life's challenges over the past 25 years with this special friend. Years ago, as I battled through some bouts of depression, she could hear the tone of my voice on the phone and just *know* that I needed her help. I was free to be the most pitiful and vulnerable version of "me" and she was good with that. As was I with her during her times of need.

Fortunately, I am still free to let it all hang out with this friend, without concerns of being judged. We don't get to see each other often because we live in different cities, but I know that I can call her any time of the night, if I need to, and she will do whatever she can to walk me through my mess. *"A man of many companions may come to ruin, but there is a friend who sticks closer than a brother"* (Proverbs 18:24). A friend is someone who, in your time of crisis, you know you not only *can* call, you know she'd *want* you to.

Share your weariness with a friend. Please don't allow the enemy to speak lies to your heart that nobody cares about you. Jesus is the greatest friend you can ever have. He never tires of listening, never sleeps, is never judgmental, and He loves you unconditionally. If you are hurting right now and truly cannot think of a friend to reach out

> **Don't allow the enemy to speak lies to your heart that nobody cares about you.**

to, talk with Jesus first—and then ask Him to send you a friend "with skin on" to help support you through the fire.

One of the few "perks" of being in this marital predicament, I am learning, is that there are a lot of other hurting women out there who can relate to what I'm going through. And a sense of camaraderie and bonding comes more easily with women who are in a similar place. It's not necessarily a "club" I would have ever wanted to join, but it's an opportunity to connect on a deeper level with new friends. God knows your heart. He sees your tears. He has a special friend, or several, in place to help you walk this road which He has allowed you to walk.

SEND OUT YOUR SOS

Scripture instructs us to *"carry each other's burdens, and in this way you will fulfill the law of Christ"* (Galatians 6:2). Call on your friends. Text them. On many occasions I have sent out an SOS text to a small group of friends with a specific prayer need. Some would text back a prayer that I would reread throughout the day. If there is a certain person you feel would be helpful to talk with, but just can't make the call, ask someone closest to you to call for you.

You, perhaps, will not find a more beautiful time of experiencing the Body of Christ in action then when you reach out to a friend. There is a special blessing as well for those who come to your aid. It is a great gift for someone to know that they are needed by you. That they can intercede for you, send you a card in the mail, take you out for a cup of coffee, let you know when they've heard a song or a sermon, or read a book that could be a source of strength to you.

Allow others to be the hands and feet of Christ to encourage you and love on you without you feeling bad about it. One person I have reached out to is my sister in law. We were not especially close over the years, until now. She lost my brother to cancer several years ago and has gained a lot of wisdom and compassion for women who hurt. She is strong but she is also gifted in her ability to listen well. And she is bold enough to be honest with me in her counsel. Our circumstances are obviously different, yet she is able to identify with many of my struggles and has helped me navigate through them. This wouldn't happen if I hadn't shared my burdens.

You will have your turn to be the helping friend to someone else. God is preparing you for such a time. This may be *your* time to heal. Even if you would much prefer to be the caregiver than the one on the receiving end (trust me, I know).

It is God's design that we need each other, just as it is His design that we need Him desperately.

Chapter 18

REV UP YOUR "FUN" TANK

The author of the book of Ecclesiastes, King Solomon, was called the wisest man of his time. And he struggled just like I do with how to balance "work and play." Solomon wrote, *"So my heart began to despair over all my toilsome labor under the sun"* (Ecclesiastes 2:20). He knew that all work and no play isn't good for anyone.

Oh how I wish I could fill this chapter with a long list of creative and awesomely fun things to do which I came up with on my own. How I wish suggestions were filling my thoughts to overflowing. I stink in this department. Just ask my kids. Somewhere back in years gone by, the idea of "planning for fun" slipped off my "to do" list. And that's sad. It shouldn't be that way. It's not that I don't love having a good time. I do. I just often find myself caught up in my "serious" to do list and in taking care of other people's needs. So much so that I do a poor job of thinking and planning for "funness." But I'm ready to change that. I heard a speaker at a women's conference say that her grandmother's favorite expression was, "But we had fun, didn't we?" She sounds like a kind of woman I would love to know. I want to be the fun mother and grandmother, the fun friend, the fun co-worker.

DO YOU KNOW SOME FUN PEOPLE?

"A happy heart makes the face cheerful, but heartache crushes the spirit" (Proverbs 15:13). Having a "happy heart" sounds very appealing to me. With all the changes this year, I am finding myself in a place of needing to make new traditions and new memories. And I would love to see some cheerful smiles and happy laughter go along with all this newness. Fortunately for me, despite my low scores on planning something fun, I have done a good job of surrounding myself with friends who are *fun* people. One in particular makes sure to take pictures of our little group while we are in the moment of having fun, so that later on we can remember the adventure we were on—which makes my heart happy again!

To write this chapter, I have sent out an SOS to some of my fun friends to help me come up with suggestions to share with you on how to have fun. Here goes a rather random "fun" list for you to consider experiencing with a friend. Grab a highlighter and mark some you'd like to try this week.

FUN ADVENTURES WITH LITTLE TO NO PLANNING

- Load up your bikes and find a bike trail or a road less traveled. Pack a lunch to enjoy along the way. Go for the cardio workout or better yet, go for a pace which will allow you to enjoy good conversation.
- Head downtown on a Saturday morning to window shop and get a cup of coffee.
- Go see a matinée movie and do an early dinner.
- Get outdoors and go for a hike. Try a new trail which neither of you have hiked.
- Enjoy a lunch or dinner out at some place new. Consider ordering something you haven't tried before.
- Visit an art museum.
- Go antique shopping, garage sale exploring, or Goodwilltreasure hunting.

- Mall walk on a rainy day.
- Try canoeing or kayaking or riding horses.

FUN ADVENTURES WITH SOME PLANNING

- Sign up for a "ladies night out" event at your church (or a friend's church).
- Commit to a women's weekend retreat months in advance, so you can save up and look forward to it.
- Go to a concert or a theatre play.
- Take a course at a nearby campus that you both have an interest in.
- Sign up for a pottery or painting or cooking class. Find a new hobby and give it a try.
- Plan a day trip to a place you have never visited or even an overnight stay in a Bed and Breakfast.
- Accomplish a big task you've been putting off (painting a room,etc.)
- Call a friend who lives out of town and invite yourself over for an overnight visit. Really. She won't mind. Reciprocate the invite the next time.
- Put it on your calendar to meet together to walk (and talk) every week. Or skip the walking and schedule a weekly coffee date. "And let us consider how we can spur one another on toward love and good deeds. Let us not give up meeting together, as some are in the habit of doing, but let us encourage one another—and all the more as you see the Day approaching (Hebrews 10:24-25)."

FUN ADVENTURES COMBINED WITH SERVING OTHERS
Here is advice which comes from a friend whose walk with Jesus I have admired for years. She says, "Consider this: Although I am in a unique category (betrayed, abandoned, divorced, separated, single mom), it does not exempt me from serving and ministering to others. I can use my gifts and resources to help others." There is

certainly healing that takes place when we look outside of our own needs and help those who are hurting.

Yesterday, joined by four sweet friends, we visited an addiction recovery facility where I help with a Christmas program every year. We sang carols, shared God's Word, and fellowshipped with the men and women who were in the program there. It was so much more rewarding and enjoyable experiencing this event with friends. The five of us traveled home together, sharing ways we had been blessed that morning. (And, I might add, we ended the trip with a visit to a dairy farm on the way home to buy some home-made goodies and, of course, to take our picture with the cows! Did you know their tongues are long enough to clean inside their nostrils? It's the most fun I've had in a long time!)

Serving others helps to keep our personal "woes" in perspective, as we see the bigger picture of living life in a fallen world.

Here are a few more suggestions:

- Volunteer at a food bank or a soup kitchen.
- Sign up to do Meals on Wheels and stay to visit a shut-in.
- Research volunteer opportunities in your city or church, and commit to one.

What do YOU desire to do? Not just what are you obligated to do. What are the desires of your heart? If you find yourself in a place that you haven't given that question a thought in a long time, then take a moment now and ask God to reveal the desires of your own heart to you. It will be His great pleasure to help!

"There is time for everything, and a season for every activity under heaven...a time to weep and a time to laugh, a time to mourn and a time to dance" (Ecclesiastes 3:1,4). And a time to *choose* to find joy in this journey and have some FUN!

Chapter 19

WORRIED ABOUT WHAT TO SAY? GOD'S GOT YOU COVERED

There is a great deal of stress that works its way into a home when there is disunity in a marriage, no matter what the cause of the discord. Arguments, accusations, insults, and then facing the complete unknown of the days ahead—all can rob you of your peace. Through every part of this process of my marriage unraveling, I have needed to respond to a lot of questions. Questions which have come from my spouse, my kids, my extended family, and friends. And some questions have come from those I don't even know so well.

I have had to anticipate some really hard conversations while my head and heart vacillate all over the place. What if I ramble on and say too much? If I answer without careful thought, I have the potential to do a lot of harm. Words that might leave me with great regret for having said them. A few folks are just nosy, but I have found that most people truly care. Yet what am I going to say when people ask me questions?

Literally, I could stay up all night playing out various responses in my head. I could worry about how my words might come out of my mouth or how they might be received. Then I am reminded of one of my favorite verses from the book of Philippians. *"Don't worry about anything; instead, pray about everything; tell God your needs, and don't forget to thank Him for His answers. If you do this, you will experience God's peace, which is far more wonderful than the human mind can understand. His peace will keep your thoughts and your hearts quiet and at rest as you trust in Christ Jesus"* (Philippians 4:6-7 TLB). Don't worry. Instead pray. Why is that so often the last thing I remember to do?

SAY WHAT GOD GIVES YOU TO SAY

Scripture also says that worrying doesn't add a single hour to our life (Matthew 6:27). For real. Not a single good thing comes from staying up worrying about what we're going to say to someone, or how what we say might be received. Is there a way not to stress over it? Here's a passage worth reading, meditating on, and memorizing so we can put it into action.

> **Not a single good thing comes from staying up worrying about what we're going to say.**

It has allowed me to fall asleep on nights I could have chosen to stay awake and role-play the next day's conversation over and over again.

"Do not worry beforehand about what to say. Just say whatever is given (by God) at the time, for it is not you speaking, but the Holy Spirit" (parentheses mine) (Mark 13:11). There it is again: "Don't worry." Offer a prayer such as, *Father, I need you. Lead me in the coming hours in every decision, phone call, word I speak so that You will never be dishonored, and through it all, be glorified. Guard my tongue and speak through me. I don't know what I need to say.*

It is certainly a step of faith not to have every response prepared in advance before having a difficult conversation with someone. Sometimes it makes me feel more in control when I think I know how my talk will go because I have planned out every word. But this puts my confidence in myself and not in God. The prophet Isaiah says *"in quietness and trust"* is where we find our strength (Isaiah 30:15). I think the contrast to this would be "use lots of loud words and rely on yourself to get you through."

When we have a relationship with the Lord and are choosing to walk with Him, we can trust Him to give us just the words we need to speak at just the right time. That's what abiding in Christ looks like. It's what happens when we ask the Holy Spirit to speak through us. So don't worry. Instead pray. Trust and let God do the talking through you.

Chapter 20

RESPOND IN PRAYER -
NOT IN RETALIATION
IT'S ALWAYS OUR CHOICE TO PRAY

I'm telling you to love your enemies.
Let them bring out the best in you, not the worst.
When someone gives you a hard time,
respond with the energies of prayer,
for then you are working out of your true selves,
your God created selves.
MATTHEW 5:44 TM

But I say to you, love your enemies,
bless those who curse you,
do good to those who hate you,
and pray for those who spitefully use and persecute you.
MATTHEW 5:44 NKJV

It is always in our power, our choice, to pray for our spouse (or ex-spouse). If you have been experiencing a season that has had you feeling "powerless," then consider this privilege to pray as a great blessing. Praying for my husband has not been an easy thing to do, and honestly prior to writing this chapter, it hasn't been something I have even given much thought to do. I've done a lot of praying, just not for him! Why should I pray for the person who has caused me so much pain?

Because "the Bible tells me so" is reason enough for me to lift up my husband before the Lord. But as we look further at Scripture, we will find many *benefits* for those of us who choose to pray for our spouse. Let's look at our role model.

JESUS IS OUR ULTIMATE EXAMPLE

Jesus is our ultimate example, the One who prayed for His crucifiers as He hung on the cross. He said, *"Father, forgive them for they know not what they do"* (Luke 23:34). We are called to be imitators of Christ. How can I not pray for an "enemy" when I was a former enemy myself? Indeed, it is a privilege to be able to come into the presence of God and talk to Him about the man who I shared my life with for years.

When I pray, I ask that God would make His will be mine. Praying brings me close to the Spirit of Christ, conforming me to His image. This is in complete contrast to me continually focusing on wishing ill-will and revenge on my husband. Some days the temptation is certainly there, but I'd rather stay determined not to let myself go there. Just like slander and sarcasm, it may feel good for a brief moment. But it will tarnish my heart for much longer. How much better to pray for a changed life for the one who hurt you.

So how are we to pray? Months ago, I prayed: *Lord, help me to learn more of Your character as You lead me to pray for my husband. This is difficult to do, Father, yet You are asking me to pray. Please show me how.*

God continually reminds me in His Word with this. It's *"not by might nor by power, but by my Spirit"* (Zechariah 4:6) that I am enabled to forgive and pray. The Holy Spirit helps us pray for the ability to show kindness to our offender. God knows we cannot do this on our own!

Begin by telling the Lord that, apart from Him, you know you don't have it in you to pray. When we choose to pray for our spouse, we are extending the grace God has given us. We are expressing kindness. Kindness helps remove stumbling blocks which could be hindering our spouse's faith walk (2 Corinthians 6:3,6). I don't want my tone of voice or bitter facial scowling to cause anyone to be turned off to Jesus. In 1 Peter 2:15 says that in responding with kindness and *"doing good"* we might *"silence the ignorant talk of foolish people."* It is God's will that by choosing to do good, we hush the nonsense talk of people who find fault with us. I can pray hard and I can focus on doing the next good thing, whatever that may be. What others have heard about me or choose to think about me is not in my control. I love the freedom in that.

There have been too many conversations over the past year with my spouse that have circled round and round regarding wrongful accusations toward me to *ever* think my spoken words can change a calloused heart. I'd rather take the better approach to the mess in my marriage, overpowering evil with good rather than attempting to retaliate and get even. Who knows, being kind may lead my offender to repentance. I must pray for him.

HOW ARE WE TO PRAY?

Joe Carter (*The Gospel Coalition*, August 14, 2014) wrote of ways we are to pray for our enemies. I think they are excellent and worth sharing. Begin by praying for your spouse's salvation, or for his return to walking out his faith. Pray that he will feel sincere regret about his sin and be able to receive forgiveness from God. Pray that the evil he does may be restrained. This may include praying restraint against hurt that could come from future lying and deceit, especially if there are children involved. This last suggestion is a tricky one. We are to pray that he will receive divine justice from God, yet we are to be very careful that our motives in this are pure.

"Do not repay anyone evil for evil. Be careful to do what is right

in the eyes of everyone. If it is possible, as far as it depends on you, live at peace with everyone. Do not take revenge, *my dear friends, but leave room for God's wrath"* (Romans 12:17-19). Leave vengeance to God. Carter says that we are to save this prayer as our last resort if the person refuses to turn to God, or to turn away from doing evil. I don't have to understand how all that works, I just know that I am supposed to pray and try to be kind. God will be God.

When we ask God to help us let the past go, *"forgetting what lies behind and straining toward what is ahead"* (Philippians 3:13), we put ourselves in a better position to pray for our spouse. It is hard to sincerely pray for someone we feel sheer bitterness toward. Again, this is something we are incapable of doing on our own strength. God wants to help us with this. *"Set your hope fully on the grace that will be brought to you at the revelation of Jesus Christ. As obedient children, do not be conformed to the passions of your former ignorance, but as he who called you is holy, you also be holy in your conduct"* (1 Peter 1:14-15 ESV). Yes, we are to stand up for our rights and our protection but we are not to retaliate, for the motive in retaliation is vengeance, and the felt benefits are only short lived.

BE A WARRIOR FOR KINGDOM GOOD

I'm not sure how best to describe it, but something happens when I pray for my husband. There is joy in knowing that as I pray, God will use my prayers for Kingdom good.

> **I feel God's favor on me when I am able to bring my spouse's needs to the throne in prayer.**

I no longer feel like a victim, but rather a warrior. It shows me how far God has brought me through this fire and how much He is growing my heart. I have not been burned and consumed. It make me feel as if Isaiah 40:31 was written just for me: *"But those who hope in the Lord will renew their strength. They will* soar *on wings like eagles."* When I pray, I find hope. Hope binds my thoughts together with God's thinking. My confidence and trust shifts to His "ableness" and I soar. When I pray, it redirects my thoughts and my hope toward the future, and the good I know the Lord has in store for me (Jeremiah 29:11).

Without a doubt, I can say that the betrayal I've experienced has tested my faith more than it has probably been tested before. God is allowing me to taste and see that indeed this testing of my faith has developed in me perseverance and *"perseverance must finish its work so that [I] may be mature and complete, not lacking anything"* (James 1:4). James says we are to consider this pure joy. I am able to continue on, in spite of difficulties. Pure joy. How sweet is that?

Job was a blameless and upright man of God, yet great devastation was allowed to fall on him and his family. Job had some friends who did a lousy job of standing by him as his life came unraveled. They actually blamed Job for the trials he experienced. But God allowed Job to soar. *"After Job had prayed for his friends the Lord made him prosperous again and gave him twice as much as he had before"* (Job 42:10). Job's prayer marked a turning point back to his success. Isn't God good?

There is so much more God desires for us to glean from our trials than to just "get through" the mess. When we allow God to work in our hearts, and through our words and actions, the result is praise, glory, and honor for all of us to experience. Everyone we come in contact with, including our spouse, can taste of God's presence and power as He lifts us up out of the pit and helps us to stand tall. And on those days when we're able to pray for the one who's hurt us, He helps us to soar above the grip of the enemy.

Chapter 21

WAIT ON GOD WHEN
HE TELLS YOU TO WAIT

THE BEST EXAMPLE I KNOW
OF **NOT** WAITING

Just over ten years ago, we brought our daughter (child number four) home from China. Adoption was something we felt God had placed on our hearts to do, and after completing a LOT of paperwork, this precious and petite 25-month-old became part of our forever family. The process took twenty-two months to complete from beginning to end. It was such an amazing experience to adopt a child from the other side of the world, and from the moment we saw her we already loved her so much.

Within two months of having Cooper home with us, I sensed another tugging on my heart to consider doing a second adoption. With a little convincing, my husband was on board. We both felt we had so much to offer another child. So by the third month of Cooper being home with us, we had completed the paperwork for another little girl, this time from Guatemala.

There was word that the country would be closing its doors to international adoptions at the end of the year, which gave us only a few months to complete the adoption. Because we were looking for a girl, as well as a girl close in age to our recently adopted two-year-old, this narrowed the number of children available. The task at hand was looking more challenging.

As usual, I was journaling throughout those weeks. I remember as if it were yesterday, when I wrote "Wait on Me, Kirby" at the top of that day's journal. I had written out my concerns to the Lord about how this thing could possibly work out when the time frame it needed to take place in was literally running out! The agency we were using at the time was the same wonderful agency we had used for our China adoption.

There was nothing further on my end I could do but wait and see if a girl could be found for us through the team of people our agency was using. The agency said "give it time" and God said "wait."

I didn't wait. I didn't keep my trust fixed on the Lord. I stayed up for hours at my computer late into the night, and by golly, I found some possibilities that just might help this adoption thing work out. In the middle of the night, I left emails for four different adoption agencies to please give me a call ASAP. Within just a few short days, I had chosen a new agency and quickly completed all their necessary paperwork. And I had wired a very large check necessary to "seal the deal" for them to get started.

It still makes me rather sick to my stomach to say what happened next. Within two hours of me "sealing the deal" with this random agency who held out all kinds of hope, I received a call from the social worker with our first agency letting us know that a little girl (just the age we were seeking) had been located and was available.

It was as good as done. Yet because the large chunk of money needed for the adoption had already been spent, we needed to stick with Plan B, the plan I had frantically created in the wee hours of the night because it is so doggone hard to wait!

I could write an entire book on the events which took place as a result of my act of *impatience* and *disobedience* to God's "Wait on Me, Kirby" before we were finally able to complete our second adoption. Of a 5-year-old boy. From Kazakhstan. I don't really understand how God's sovereignty works.

Somehow He is still in control regardless of the choices I make, because He is God. But I am learning that His ways are not our ways. Not even close. I wouldn't trade my precious son for anything. I think in the Lord's all-knowing capacity that He knew my Plan B was how we would complete our family. Doing it my way just happened to take three years versus three months, thousands more in cash, and many, many more gray hairs.

Perhaps God allowed me to experience my Plan B so I might be a little smarter the next time He asks me to keep my eyes fixed on Him and "wait" while He meets my needs. Without a doubt, those three years were three of the most emotionally challenging years I have ever experienced...and they really didn't have to be.

I understand that any adoption process is emotional and comes with stress. Yet on this particular ride, I took my eyes off the very One who had called us to adopt. Instead of filling my "waiting" moments with TRUST, I filled them with hours of busyness and reading stories about other people's adoption journeys, many of which were unsuccessful and heartbreaking. I invested my energies in matters that would be of no benefit to me or anyone else. I tortured myself with worry, which robbed me of being able to enjoy the beautiful people I was with in *that* moment.

I'm not saying that reading up on things to educate or even entertain ourselves is wrong. But my FOCUS was wrong. For three years I lived on an exhausting emotional roller coaster, which went up and dropped down with every step forward and every step back our adoption journey would take.

Maybe God allowed me to go through that roller coaster faith ride so I'd be more prepared for *this* ride He has allowed me to be on in my marriage. I have learned that we CAN walk difficult paths which God allows in our lives when we keep our eyes fixed on Jesus and His promises. Our God never changes. His Word says that He will never leave us nor forsake us (Hebrews 13:5). We never need to walk alone. As all-knowing Creator, God sees the plans ahead of us. Yet He waits for us to acknowledge our need for Him, and call on Him.

> **We get to choose how we want to walk through the storms in our life.**

Will it be in our own strength or clinging tightly to the faithful One we can trust?

God's plan would have us asking the Lord for His direction. Then we need to LISTEN, WAIT and TRUST that God's got us covered. Does that mean the road ahead will be easy? It hasn't been for me, and I am guessing that it hasn't been an easy journey for you either.

We live in a broken world and it's not going to be trouble-free this side of eternity. We will step out at times into what feels like blind faith. *We may not know where our steps are leading, but we can know the One who leads.* God loves us more than any human being ever could.

I struggle still with waiting on those things that require me to wait. Yet when I sense that God wants me to "Wait on Me, Kirby," I am much more inclined to do so because I am learning to trust Him. If there is only confusion ahead with no apparent direction, I wait knowing that at the right time, He will show me what to do. I'm also learning that when God says it's time for me to move ahead, I need to move!

THERE'S A REASON FOR BLURRED VISION

I believe that many times God keeps the steps ahead of us cloudy and blurred for a reason. This lack of clarity on the road ahead is often the Lord's way of protecting us. The less I can see, the more I must trust. God will use whatever He chooses to draw His children near to Him. Our jobs, titles, houses, and possessions will all pass away. Our relationship with the Lord is what we can enjoy forever. Nothing else compares to walking closely with Him.

Those "valleys" we experience when the chaos and conflict seem overwhelming, when we don't see how on earth we can ever move forward, often make room for our times of greatest closeness with God. This is what He desires for us each and every day. To wake up with a dependence on Him to walk closely beside us.

Ten years ago, I couldn't see how we could possibly complete our second adoption with the time running out. I was unable to trust that the agency would do everything possible to make things happen. Most importantly, I was unable to trust the instructions God spoke to my heart: "Wait on Me." I should have applied Solomon's words in Proverbs 3:5, *"Trust in the Lord with all your heart and lean not on your own understanding; In all your ways acknowledge him, and he will make your paths straight."*

When we are required to walk through what seems impossible, we have to trust He will see us through those circumstances. It is in those times, when God Himself empowers us to stand and walk the path He has called us to walk, that we are *doing* the impossible. We are walking on water. The key is learning to keep our focus fixed on Jesus. His vision is never blurred.

Chapter 22

THE SECRET TO WALKING ON WATER

I don't think there is a story in the Bible that better illustrates where our focus needs to be as we walk through life than in Matthew 14:27-36. Jesus' disciples find themselves in a small boat on a lake, far from the shore, in the middle of the night, in a storm. They are scared. Their fear only escalates when they see what they think is a ghost walking toward them on the water. It's no ghost—it"s Jesus!

> But Jesus immediately said to them: 'Take courage! It is I. Don't be afraid.' 'Lord, if it is you,' Peter replied, 'tell me to come to you on the water.' 'Come,' he said. Then Peter got down out of the boat, **walked on water** and came toward Jesus. But when he **saw the wind** he was afraid and, beginning to sink, cried out, 'Lord, save me!' Immediately Jesus reached out his hand and caught him. 'You of little faith,' he said, 'why did you doubt?' And when they climbed into the boat, the wind died down. Then those who were in the boat worshiped him, saying, 'Truly you are the Son of God.'

The moment Peter took his eyes off Jesus, his focus shifted to the raging winds and the swirling dark waters beneath, and Peter began to sink.

IT'S ALL ABOUT FOCUS

What makes the difference between walking on water and "going under" lies in where we choose to keep our focus. Our goal is to walk through life's storms without letting our circumstances drown or consume us. The goal of the enemy is to take us down and hold us there—to suck the life out of God's children and make them believe that the fight is over and all hope is gone.

Is it really possible to walk the impossible? Nowhere do the Scriptures tell us that our lives will be without storms or disappointments. Rather, Jesus said, *"In this world you will have trouble. But take heart, I have overcome the world"* (John 16:31).

Some days we may get the wind knocked out of us when a hard wave hits. But we can always get back up again and walk in confidence, because the Scriptures say we never walk alone. *"The Lord himself goes before you and will be with you; he will never leave you nor forsake you. Do not be afraid. Do not be discouraged"* (Deuteronomy 31:8). It is through Christ's grace, mercy, and power that we are able to journey through our challenges victoriously. Not our own strength.

WHAT'S IN A CHAPTER'S TITLE?

The Holy Spirit equips each of us to trust God's promises and to obey them. Our part is to diligently work at keeping our focus on God and His faithfulness, moment by moment. Take a minute to turn back to the Table of Contents of this book and read the chapter titles slowly. (Go ahead. I'll wait.) These are all OUR part; things which, with God's help, we can choose to work on. Keeping the right focus is hard work!

Just a few months ago I journaled, *Jesus, I'm grieving. I'm tired of looking back at all the mess and pain I've been through, yet I'm feeling overwhelmed as I look forward. There's a lot to keep up with, take care of, be responsible for. Give me Your strength to do the things I need to do. I see clearly that I cannot take any more steps without You walking by my side, without You going before me to prepare the way. Jesus, help me. I am weary and filled with doubt.*

It's fair to say that I was starting to sink. It's also fair to say that it will probably not be the last time I find myself bobbing up and down for air.

God already knows when we are feeling stressed and riddled with fear from our circumstances. Fear comes when we believe that God's not big enough to handle our mess. His answer to our unbelief is that we keep our eyes and ears on Him and on His promises. He is the faithful One.

> **He is ready to walk hand in hand with us when we call on His name.**

When we choose to keep our focus on the Lord, He helps to quiet our minds of worry and unnecessary concerns. Quieting my mind means less talking, less texting, less interaction with people, and more making myself be still with the Lord.

The saddest words in the book of Job are seen in Job 3:36, *"I have no peace, no quietness: I have no rest, but only turmoil."* Job's trials had become all consuming, and he felt hopeless. My experiences have not come close to the afflictions Job endured, but I have tasted those words early in my own trials, and they are almost unbearable. The enemy had worked hard to take my marriage, and I knew he wanted much more.

DO YOU REALLY WANT YOUR THOUGHTS TO GO THERE?
What we think on, we can become. *"For as a man thinks in his heart, so is he"* (Proverbs 23:7). Those things on which we choose to focus, the places we allow our mind to go, have a huge influence on our lives. Do I really need to pore over Facebook to know

the whereabouts of certain people at certain times? Is that helpful to my heart? Does listening to slanderous talk from others about people once near to me benefit anyone at all? Does anything good come of it? What I allow to occupy my thoughts, in time, will determine my speech and my actions.

The apostle Paul writes, *"Whatever is true (not lies of the world), whatever is noble (worthy of my respect), whatever is right (just), whatever is pure, whatever is lovely, whatever is admirable—if anything is excellent or praiseworthy—think about such things...and the God of peace will be with you"* (parentheses mine) (Philippians 4:8-9). I have memorized and used these verses on many occasions to counter "bad" thoughts that were working to take up residence in my head. As I speak them aloud one phrase at a time, such as "whatever is true," I ask God to remind me of His truth, such as, "I am a daughter of the King. I belong to him. I am forgiven." Then I move to the next word, "noble" and begin to make a mental list of some of those things and people in my life who are worthy of my respect, and I thank God for them. As I work my way through the list, my mind is able to get back on focus and the "yuk" that had been knocking at my brain starts fading away.

We should have a healthy respect for God. When God says through His Word, or His Spirit speaking to your heart, that you need to do something—then trust Him and do what He says immediately. Delayed obedience is *dis*-obedience. He is making a way for us, and we need to follow! We need to keep our eyes on Jesus because He is bigger than any storm we might face. Yet if we forget to trust, we can cry out like Peter did *("Lord, save me")* and be assured that God's hand is there and He has taken hold.

I'll end this chapter with a Hillsong song, "Spirit Lead Me," which I heard for the first time last year when the waters around me were raging. Take a minute and see if you can pull it up on the internet and let the words and music minister to your heart as you and the Lord walk on the waters together. The chorus of the song encourages us to call on the Lord as He leads us into waters that are too great for us to handle on our own. Oh that our faith would be made stronger each time our faith is being challenged as our soul rests in Jesus.

Chapter 23

RUN YOUR RACE TO WIN THE PRIZE
OUR PAST? GOD'S NOT THERE

No one can run a race well with their eyes looking behind them. It's doesn't make for very effective running. God's desire is for us to walk with Him fully in the moment, one day at a time. Seeking the preciousness of our *now,* even in those painful moments. God does not reside in our past, nor should we. *"Forgetting the past and looking forward to what lies ahead, I strain to reach the end of the race and receive the price for which God is calling us up to heaven because of what Christ Jesus did for us"* (Philippians 3:13-14 TLB).

"Get into the game and stop looking back." "This is your now." "Prepare yourself to move forward." "Get your game face on and be determined to win." Man, those phrases sound enthusiastic, but I don't have it in me to think like that. I'm still wounded. Yet, I *can* do it through Christ. I can do all things through Christ *in* me!

We break the power of our past, which is something we can't change, by not living in the past, but rather by living for our future, which is something we *can* change. If you had anger and hurtful words targeted at you in the past, and you remember how that left

Satan loses when we use his hurt for God's good. you feeling hurt and worthless— use that memory to avoid doing the same to someone else. Break the cycle. Satan loses when we use his hurt for God's good. Don't pay the insults forward. When you do say something hurtful that you wish you hadn't, ask for forgiveness and move on. Learn from your past hurts and be better for them.

"Do you not know that in a race all the runners run, but only one gets the prize? Run in such a way as to get the prize...do it to get a crown that will last forever" (1 Corinthians 9:24-25). We don't run our race well in order to earn our way into Heaven. Salvation cannot be bought. Jesus took care of that when He offered his life on the cross for us. Our belief in who Christ is, and what He did for us, is the source of our salvation. During the time when Paul penned the book of Corinthians, the Greek athletic games had only one winner for each event. Only one could win the crown. Today *every* follower of Christ can win a crown or reward when he stands before the Lord one day. The crown is to hear the Lord say, *"Well done, good and faithful servant!"* (Matthew 25:21) He created us to bring our Creator glory and to please Him.

IS THIS YOUR CROSSROAD?

How do we measure how well we are running this race? One of my favorite speakers, Ruth McWhite, taught me this at a women's retreat. Whenever we hit a crossroad in life where the "rubber meets the road," where we must determine whether what we do and say are going to line up with what we think we believe, then we need to consider: How am I going to bring God glory in this?

Writing this book has continually challenged me to answer that question. As I was studying and writing the chapter on forgiveness, I found myself at a crossroad every time I got my feelings hurt and resentment began to grow. Was I going to forgive and continue my race to please God? Or was I going to allow myself to sit at that crossroad far too long while I had an ugly pity party? We will con-stantly be challenged and tested to do what is right and pleasing to the Lord. Ruth says we are to ask ourselves, "How do I measure if I looked like Jesus yesterday? Today? Did I show love? Did I feel joy? Did I experience peace? Did I show kindness?" Is my faith growing stronger as it becomes a greater challenge to believe God? To see God? This is how we bring God glory.

Our goal in this race called life is this: *To fight the good fight. To finish the race. To keep the faith* (from 2 Timothy 4:7). Sadly, I am not able to save my marriage. But I *can* run this race in a way that makes my heavenly Father proud. And there is incredible joy and purpose in such a journey! As much as God hates divorce, I will be bold enough to say that it is not always God's best to choose to stay in a marriage. The question to ask is: Will the road I choose ultimately bring God glory? With the strength of the Holy Spirit that indwells every believer, we can choose to walk closely with God. We can be determined to persevere.

"Blessed is the man who perseveres under trial, for when he has stood the test, he will receive the crown of life that God has promised to those who love him" (James 1:12). Whatever that "crown" might look like, seeing the smile on my Savior's face one day because I fought this fight and ran this race in a   God-honoring way will be worth it all. Because God is who I get to spend my eternity with and THAT marriage will last forever.

IS YOUR FAITH "BIGGER THAN"?
Perhaps our biggest obstacle in running this race is FEAR. "Let Your Faith be Bigger Than Your Fear" is a plaque that looks back at me each time I stand at my kitchen sink. The words are key for this race. Fear is not of God, but faith is. Over and over in Scripture, God's Word tells us not to fear, for fear will sink us.

Fear not, for I have redeemed you; [Put your own name

here], I have summoned you by name; you are mine. When you pass through the waters, I will be with you; and when you pass through the rivers, they will not sweep over you. When you walk through the fire, you will not be burned; the flames will not set you ablaze. For I am the Lord your God of Israel, your Savior (Isaiah 43:1-3).

These God-inspired words in Isaiah have been breathing life into me the past two years, through every river of difficulty and fire of oppression I have faced. When you and I walk through situations that are challenging, when we can't see where our feet are stepping or where the path is going, God will always be with us. And He knows the way!

I have seen many fires and experienced moments when the heat seemed more than I could bear, and the air felt devoid of oxygen to breathe. But I was not burned up. I came through it whole. My trials did not destroy me, nor will the trials yet to come. In the Lord, I am an overcomer. The Lord God my Savior has carried me and shielded me from harm. Each time I remember the fires which God and I have already been through, my faith is made stronger and my gratitude is greater. I know that I am His precious child.

I must say, I still wish I didn't have to walk this road in the first place. This was never the way I dreamed my life would be. Yet as I run this race, because of the One who runs beside me (and sometimes has to *carry* me), I can now run with eager anticipation of what the Lord has in store for me. And it is well with my soul.

Chapter 24

USE YOUR TRIALS
TO POINT OTHERS TO JESUS
HOW WILL YOU RESPOND?

I have another decorative plaque in my kitchen that reads…

Life isn't about waiting for the storm to pass,
it's about learning to dance in the rain.

I like to think when we're able to sing God's praises and press on through the storm, with hope—then we are dancing on the inside. And when the clouds are their darkest, with no forecast of sun, we can know that people are watching hard for our response. Our response in times of adversity is perhaps the truest indicator of who we really are and what we believe.

This is our "crossroad." Our opportunity to let Jesus shine. Like a full moon (or as pastor Louie Giglio calls it, a "big ball of dirt") which has no source of light in and of itself. The way the moon is positioned toward the Sun reflects the Sun's light toward earth. It's the Sun's brightness, not the moon's darkness, we see. How will we respond? Who will we choose to reflect through our trials?

Elisabeth Elliot, in her book *Be Still My Soul,* writes this. "What counts the most is our response to everything. It is not what happens to us, but how we respond and how we look to God for strength and guidance." Will we reflect the Son?

A sister quote to the earlier one about dancing in life's storms is a quote, which for reasons long forgotten by me, I chose as the quote to accompany my yearbook senior picture.

When life gives you lemons, make lemonade.

Life often seems to come with sour lemons and some rain. This is the question we need to ask ourselves. Are we going to wait until the storms pass and our circumstances "sweeten" before we feel like we are truly living? Will we believe that only then God is able to use us for something of purpose? Am I going to allow the enemy to keep my mouth shut about the good things that God is doing? The deceiver wants me to think that since my marriage has failed, I'm all washed up and finished. That because I am flawed (and we are ALL flawed), somehow God can't use me.

Yet you and I are useable by God NOW. Even if the only thing we have strength to do is call out, "Jesus, help me!", we are still pointing others to Christ. We all need to be reminded of where to turn for help. We can see this in Psalm 121:1-2 when the psalmist writes, *"I lift up my eyes to the hills—where does my help come from? My help comes from the Lord, the Maker of heaven and earth."* We can tell others our story of where our help comes from. God is faithful to His promises. Always. Someone needs to know.

WHAT IS A HAPPY-EVER-AFTER ENDING?

Early on, when I first experienced the shock of learning there had been a breach of trust in my marriage, and that so much of what I had believed to be true in our relationship was a lie, I knew I needed to talk with someone. I wanted to talk with women who had been through what I was going through. But only to those who had experienced a "success" story with a happy ever-after ending. Success to me, at that time, only meant that the marriage was restored and flourishing. I reminded God that if our family and friends witnessed my 35 year marriage being saved, it would make Him look really amazing. He had raised Lazarus from the dead, and I knew He could raise what seemed to be beyond restoration in my marriage as well.

Now I know that a true happy ending, though a sad means to the end, is a story where others see Jesus walking beside me at the beginning, through the pitfalls in the middle, to the very end of this fire-filled journey. A happy or blessed path is one which enables us to point those who are watching to Jesus. Because of how we choose to respond to our circumstances. When we allow God to make something good and sweet out of the bitter things in life, we are reflecting God's Son.

COMFORTED TO COMFORT OTHERS

Another way we point people to Jesus is by offering comfort to those who hurt. Remember, we are not here for ourselves. If God calls us to walk a difficult path, He will walk closely beside us. And His grace will be sufficient for us to pour out onto those He places on our hearts. All of us seek to be comforted by someone or something. I love how *The Living Bible* says this in 2 Corinthians 1:3-4.

What a wonderful God we have –he is the Father of our Lord Jesus Christ, the source of every mercy, and the one who so wonderfully comforts and strengthens us in our hardships and trials. And why does he do this? So that when others are troubled, needing our sympathy and encouragement, we can pass onto them this same help and comfort God has given us.

Comforting others may come by way of us meeting a practical need for a hurting friend, such as bringing chocolate or coffee or a meal. I got all of the above. You might send her an encouraging note or Bible verse. I received many. It might be a text or call to let them know they are on your mind and you are praying for them. I think God knows when His sheep need comforting, and He often prompts other sheep to come alongside the hurting at just the right time. When we strengthen someone, we comfort them.

As wonderful as it feels to receive comfort, Scripture doesn't say God's chief concern is for His children to be comfortable. He loves us too much to let us stay comfortable. Rather He offers us a way for all our circumstances to produce "good." God chooses to use ALL things, including our suffering, to *"work for the good of those who love him, who have been called according to his purpose"* (Romans 8:28). "Good" is not always the happy ending we had hoped for.

It did not feel "good" when the pediatrician came into my hospital room after my son's birth to tell me he had Down syndrome. I would not have chosen the more challenging road of parenting a child with disabilities. Yet I would not trade all that the Lord continues to teach me, and many others, through my son.

Good is not always feeling comfortable. Rather, it is when God begins to conform us into the likeness of Jesus Christ. It is when we are able to reflect and radiate Christ in our circumstances. No matter what those circumstances happen to be.

Good is when we live at such a level of dependence on the Lord that His strength is what is exhibited through us.

Moment by moment. God even loves us enough to keep us dependent on Him through our suffering.

Alone we can't muster up the strength to press through our

suffering. Yet when we ABIDE in Christ, we can stand. And often we can even soar! When others begin to see some "good" come from our bad, this good gives glory to the Father.

For those who are dear to me who say they don't believe this Jesus is real, there is no denying that what they're seeing as they watch me walk through this fire, is *not* me. IT IS JESUS IN ME! And He is real. If those I love have a chance to believe because they see Jesus in me—then I can count all my trials as mere "rubbish" that they may gain Christ.

OUR POINT OF VIEW MAKES ALL THE DIFFERENCE

From a human perspective, there is no joy in the losses my family has faced. Nor in the losses we will face in the future. Because of the events which have happened in this marriage, upcoming holidays, graduations, and weddings of our younger kids, birth of grandkids—none of this will *ever* look quite as I'd hoped it would. That is a loss. A big one. Yet our point of view, our perspective, can still make all the difference in how we see our suffering.

Whose eyes are we going to see our circumstances through? Is God good? Is He in control? Does He use all things for good to those who love Him? Does God have plans to prosper us and bring us a hope and a future? Is His grace sufficient to meet our every need? *Yes, yes, and yes!*

God is faithful to exchange those *earthly* things lost in the fire we've endured with more wonderful *heavenly* things. *Allow yourself to know that this is true.* Yes, beloved daughter of the King, your Father in Heaven is good. He loves you more than anyone else ever could.

Ask the Lord to help you look outside yourself and see how you might pass this hope onto others. As you do, you begin to find special purpose in your pain. You begin to see that Jesus alone will satisfy whatever it is you're looking for. When we draw from God's comfort and choose to see our circumstances from a heavenly perspective, restoration is taking place. Receiving comfort and giving it away—this is the body of Christ in action. And it is alive and beautiful. Every "fiery" trial God has allowed me to experience has opened my eyes to this reality. We live in a hurting, broken world. And this short time here on planet earth "ain't it." We are just passing through on our way Home.

USE THOSE HEELS TO STOMP!
"The God of peace will soon crush Satan under your feet" (Romans 16:20).

You know the best thing, the biggest bonus about accepting our assignment of pointing others to Jesus through our mess? The *added* prize to knowing God is working good and not wasting what we are going through? Here it is...and it is BIG. And it doesn't matter whether we are wearing our running shoes or a pair of stiletto heels.

You and I are raising our foot and striking our heel hard onto Satan's ugly head. We are striking his head every time *we look to Jesus in faith,* instead of looking at our trials. I am stomping on the same deceiver who, in the past, has stood nipping at my heels. He has been fighting hard to suck me back into the fire. This same deceiver who has tried to make me feel hopeless every time I cried out to the Lord in confusion and hurt.

But now, like the Roman soldiers who wore spiked nails on the bottom of their shoes for battle, we pound our heels against the enemy in victory! A victory which was already won when Jesus destroyed Satan's power at the cross. We are learning to walk in that victory. A celebration walk that has us cranking up the praise music, lifting our feet high, and stomping loud. Move out of the way, devil, God isn't finished here yet! Satan knows we walk in victory when we allow God to turn our defeats into triumphs. And there are many more triumphs to come.

I will leave you with words (loosely taken) from a Casting Crowns song, passed onto me from a fellow sojourner...

Your world's not falling apart, my friend.
It's falling into place.
Gradually and in God's timing.
God is so good.

24 IMPORTANT QUESTIONS

Are you continuing to feel the overwhelming "burn" of your circumstances? Then prayerfully ask yourself the following questions to see where you may need to invest some time and make some changes. Refer back to the chapter which is listed with each question to be reminded of the tools God has for you to walk in victory!

Chapter 1 - Am I choosing to walk this moment in absolute surrender to God?

Chapter 2 - Am I spending time alone with Jesus?

Chapter 3 - Is there something I need to do today that could help begin to restore a relationship in my life?

Chapter 4 - Do I need to slow down, take a deep breath, and refocus?

Chapter 5 - Have I been writing my prayer requests down, expressing my emotions on paper? Writing out what God seems to be speaking to my heart?

Chapter 6- Might I benefit from spending more time in my "prayer closet"? Am I praying each week with my prayer partner?

Chapter 7- Am I investing adequate time in God's Word and finding counsel there? Do I need to seek professional help?

Chapter 8 - Do I need to drop my "rocks" of resentment and forgive someone today?

Chapter 9 - When was the last time I cranked up the praise music and worshipped?

Chapter 10 - How am I doing on guarding my tongue from unwholesome talk and from speaking words which tear others down?

Chapter 11 - Am I being gentle with myself and allowing myself moments to grieve?

Chapter 12 - Am I learning to work on peacefully resolving conflict between me and others or am I just trying to keep the peace?

Chapter 13 - Am I acting wisely in the way I am choosing to be in relationship with others? Am I keeping my integrity?

Chapter 14 - When was the last time I wrote down my blessings and thanked God for them?

Chapter 15 - How am I doing on limiting my time with negative and or "not healthy for me" people?

Chapter 16 - What do I know to be true that would help me to heal, yet I continue not to step out and do it?

Chapter 17 - Have I been isolating myself from my friends? Would it help if I shared my struggles today with a friend?

Chapter 18 - What do I have on my calendar in the next week and month that I consider to be fun?

Chapter 19 - Is my mind worrying about what I am going to say the next time I talk to a certain person?

Chapter 20 - Have I prayed for my spouse (or my ex-spouse) today?

Chapter 21 - What might God be wanting me to hold off on/wait on? Am I waiting?

Chapter 22 - Where has my focus been today as I come up against "rough waters"?

Chapter 23 - How much time and energy am I investing in my past and the what "could have" been?

Chapter 24 - Who is someone I can shine some Jesus on and bless today? Who is someone I can pass this hope in Jesus onto this week?

When you walk through the fire you will NOT be burned; the flames will not set you ablaze. For I am the Lord, your God, the Holy One of Israel, your savior. (Isaiah 43:2-3)

APPLY IT NOW

Ready to put what you are learning into practice? If you are working through this book with others as a group, begin with Apply It Now #1 after your first group meeting. Complete each assignment before the next class meets again.

APPLY IT NOW #1 - COMPLETE BEFORE SESSION TWO
Read chapters 1-5 of *Walking Through Fire Without Getting Burned*. Highlight scripture or comments which are particularly meaningful to you. Write down any questions your reading stirs up in you. Feel free to share these during the next group meeting.

Buy a journal/composition notebook. If you presently keep a prayer journal feel free to use the one you have. Prayer journaling will be covered in more detail in a later chapter.

We will be working on growing a collection of scriptures that will serve as a source of strength and comfort for you in the days and years to come. Keep these scriptures, which you will be writing out on 3 x 5 cards, nearby. Frequently read over, and ultimately memorize these verses of promise and encouragement.

Write out Isaiah 41:13—*For I am the LORD your God who takes hold of your right hand and says to you, Do not fear; I will help you.* Read the verse aloud so your ears can hear God's promise to you. Now, turn this same verse into a prayer to speak aloud. Here's an example of praying this scripture back to God in the form of a prayer: "Lord, Your word says that You are the Lord, my God. It says that You will take hold of my right hand. You tell me not to fear, that You will help me. God, I am afraid. Help me today, not to fear and to know that You have Your hand on me. Keep reminding me that You will help me through this. Amen."

Be sure to place your card where you can see it often.

Write out Jeremiah 29:11—*For I know the plans I have for you, declares the Lord. Plans to prosper you and not to harm you. Plans to give you a hope and a future.*

Commit to spending at least 10 minutes every day this week being quiet and alone with the Lord. A good way to start may be: "Jesus help me. I cannot do this on my own. I want to run to You, Lord, before I go to others for my help. Help me to hear Your voice speaking to my heart, 'Daughter, I love you.'"

As the title of Chapter 2 says, "It Has EVERYTHING to Do With Abiding." If it is your desire to walk more intimately with the Lord and be able to enjoy Him in a real and personal way, I encourage you to read my first book, *Abiding in Christ - What Is It Anyway?*, which is available for purchase through my website, HopeforHardPlaces.com. *Abiding in Christ* will help you find the "want to" and "how to" of experiencing a closer intimacy with Jesus. Investing time in your relationship with the Lord will make all the difference in how you are able to walk through any of the fires in your life—all the difference.

APPLY IT NOW #2 - COMPLETE BEFORE SESSION THREE

Read chapter 6-8. Highlight comments that seem to speak strongly to you. Write down any questions which arise as you read, and be ready to discuss when you meet again as a group.

Read back over Matthew 5:22-24. Know that whether or not your marriage can be reconciled and fully restored is NOT in your control. Reconciliation takes two, who are both fully participating and surrendered, to have any hope for true healing. Continue to ask God to make clear to you what your part is in restoring your relationship with your spouse. If your marriage is at a place where there has been forgiveness and repentance, there is much hope! Pray for direction as to what your next step (your best next thing) needs to be. Take a step to do that this week.

Your marriage may be at the place where reconciliation is no longer an option. We will discuss in later chapters some steps you can take to make whatever relationship you may still have with your husband as healthy as possible. Are there others you have offended or who have offended you? Ask God to show you with whom you may need to seek reconciliation. Take that step this week.

Write out Isaiah 30:21 on a 3 x 5 card—*Whether you turn to the right or to the left, your ears will hear a voice behind you, saying, "This is the way; walk in it."* Read the verse aloud. Turn this into a prayer: "Lord, Your word says that whether I turn to the right or to the left my ears will hear a voice behind me saying, 'This is the way, walk in it.' God, please show me what I am to do next. Help me to walk in the way I believe You are leading me to walk. Amen." Say this verse aloud often enough until you have committed it to memory. It is a promise from God to you!

Write out Isaiah 30:15—*In repentance and rest is your salvation, in quietness and trust is your strength.* Let those two words, "quietness" and "trust" sink in. What is one thing you can do today to experience more quietness (absence of noise or business) in your day?

Turn to the prayer found in the end of Chapter 3 (under the heading of "A Profound Prayer From a Friend"). Place your name where it reads, "Kirby" and very slowly read this prayer as your own. On a 3 x 5 card, make a list of the things you are asking God for through this prayer (i.e., clarity, discernment, protection...). Use this list to guide your prayer time today and in the days to come.

Each morning and evening as you stand in front of the mirror, say aloud to yourself, "The Lord delights in me because He made me and His work is good." Repeat it again with even more confidence the second time! Please don't blow through this part of your homework just because it may feel a bit awkward. You weaken the enemy's desire to make you feel worthless each time you remind yourself of God's truths.

Take regular time outs to breathe deeply. Inhale deeply and hold 4 seconds. Exhale deeply and hold 4 seconds. Repeat 4 times. (Sometimes stress causes us to take shallow and inefficient breaths.) Consider giving a 20-30 minute YOGA class a try. This was a brand new venture for me yet surprisingly very relaxing. You may be able to borrow a DVD from a friend, the library or find a free YOGA video on Amazon Prime. Julia Jarvis has several good ones available. Take a walk and be aware of God's beauty around you.

APPLY IT NOW #3 - COMPLETE BEFORE SESSION FOUR

Read Chapters 9,10, and 11. Highlight any points of particular interest to you. Write down any questions you'd like to discuss the next time you meet with your group.

You should have the following verses of scripture written out on 3x5 cards (Isaiah 41:13, Jeremiah 29:11, Isaiah 30:21, and Isaiah 30:15). Continue to spend time each day reading over, saying aloud, and writing down each of these verses until they become part of you. Being able to recall God's Word from memory will be one of your strongest weapons of defense against the enemy.

To your collection add Isaiah 43:2-3—*Though you walk through the fire, you will not be burned; the flames will not set you ablaze. For I am the Lord, your God, the Holy One of Israel, your Savior.* Ask God to help you believe these words for your own trials today. This promise comes from the Lord and is for you.

Commit to spend at least 15 minutes each day quiet and alone with God (in prayer, reading his word and reflecting on what God has to say to you). Feel free to use the following two bullet points during this time with the Lord:

Use Chapter 7 as your guide (using a Bible concordance) to dig deeper into scripture. (Some suggestions to consider: Trust, Worry, Truth, Hope, Forgiveness, Thankfulness.) Write out at least three verses that pertain to a specific topic and highlight/mark keywords. Then write down at least one insight you've gleaned from those verses.

Paraphrase at least one (or a portion of one) of the Psalms again this week. Be sure to put it into first person and make it your personal prayer to God.

Read back over 2 Corinthians 12:9-10. Ask yourself, "Do I believe that God's grace (God's Riches at Christ's Expense) is indeed sufficient to meet all my needs today?"

Go outside and take a walk this week. Walk with no agenda except to BREATHE deeply and to enjoy the beauty in your surroundings. (This is homework!)

Stretch yourself to find a prayer partner (a woman who is willing to commit to praying with you at least once a week). Write the name of who you will ask here _____. If this is new for you, I promise the awkwardness of praying aloud with someone else will pass. Remember Matthew 18:20—*For when two or three come together in my name, there am I with them.* Give her a call today.

Write down two things you desire God to do for you this week?

Write down two things you desire God to do for your spouse this week.

Reread Matthew 18:15-35 and answer this: Who is the one person in this parable being sent to jail to be tortured? If you choose not to forgive your spouse for what he has done to hurt you (and others), who is the one (according to this passage) who is being tortured? Pray now and ask God to help you start this process of forgiveness today. This may be the biggest step in trusting God you have ever had to make. God is worthy of your trust.

APPLY IT NOW #4 - COMPLETE BEFORE SESSION 5

Read Chapters 12,13, and 14. Highlight whatever seems to speak to you in particular. Keep a list of questions that may arise as you read.

Add the following verses to your 3x5 card collection:
Philippians 4:13—*I can do all things through Christ who gives me strength.* 2 Corinthians 12:8-10—*Three times I pleaded with the Lord to take it away from me. But he said to me, "My grace is sufficient for you, for my power is made perfect in weakness." Therefore I will boast all the more gladly about my weaknesses, so that Christ's power may rest on me.*

Continue to spend time with your collection of Bible verses you are working on. (Six listed in last week's homework and two additional ones this week.)

Quiet Time: Continue being disciplined to quiet yourself with the Lord at least 15 minutes each day. Use suggestions from past homework assignments to make this time with the Lord rich and meaningful. As you continue to spend time paraphrasing the Psalms allow your pen to move from paraphrasing the psalmist's words to becoming questions and doubts and hurts you may have for God. Write them out. One day you will no longer feel the pain and emotions you are experiencing today. You do not want to forget how good and faithful Jesus has been to walk you through it. Keep a record of these moments of His faithfulness.

Finding a prayer partner: Did you ask her yet? Have you prayed together? Continue to talk to God about your specific desires. Pray with an eager anticipation for Him to answer.

Crank up the Praise Music: Write down the name of a praise song that has especially ministered to you this past year. Be prepared to sing it to the group your next time together (just kidding, unless you'd like to!). Keep the praise music playing.

Unwholesome Talk: Write out Ephesians 4:29 on a 3x5 and add it to your scripture cards listed on last week's homework—*Do not let any unwholesome talk come out of your mouths, but only what is helpful for building others up according to their needs, that it may benefit those who listen.* Turn this into your personal prayer. Ask the Holy Spirit to convict you of your unkind comments BEFORE they leave your mouth. Then bite your tongue (literally if needed) to keep them from leaving your mouth. Work hard this week to memorize this verse.

Look up Matthew 15:10-11 and write down an important reason why God wants us to bridle out tongue.

Allow Yourself a Good Cry: List 3 things you can do if you're feeling sad or overwhelmed:

1.

2.

3.

APPLY IT NOW #5 - COMPLETE BEFORE SESSION SIX

Read Chapters 15, 16, 17, and 18. Feel free to underline, highlight, and write comments by what you are reading. The more engaged you are with the text, the more you will get out of reading it.

Quiet Time: How do you feel you are doing with having intentional quiet time with God? How much time do you desire to spend in your devotional time of reading, reflecting on and memorizing scripture, praying, writing out your blessings, etc.? Write down your goal:

_____ minutes/day, _____ days/week.

Peacemaker vs. Peacekeeper: Would you call yourself a Peace-KEEPER or a peaceMAKER with your friends and acquaintances? How about with your husband? This week, ask someone else which of the two they see you as and why:

Growing up, which one of the two would you have "classified" your parents as?

Your mom?

Your dad?

Write out Matthew 5:9 on a 3x5 card—*Blessed are the peace-MAKERS, for they will be called sons of God.*

Do you believe that most of the time you do a good job of verbalizing your feelings to someone who has frustrated, angered, or disappointed you? Yes _____ No _____

List two ways you can do a better job next time you find yourself feeling this way:

1.

2.

In your own words write out what you understand to be the difference between a peacemaker and a peacekeeper:

Search the web for "peacekeeper images". This is an easier task than you may think and the image may blow your mind. Do you think this is what God has in mind for any of your relationships?

Shrewd as a Serpent: List three healthy ways you can be shrewd (wise) in your relationship with your spouse? Your kids? Or your co-workers:

1.

2.

3.

Do you think that being shrewd in a relationship indicates distrust for that person?

Should we trust a person who has previously lied to us?

Write down two practical ways that might help rebuild trust in another person:

1.

2.

Reread John Gill's description (in "Stand Up for Yourself - God's Way") for what your character should look like in your efforts to protect yourself. Circle at least three.

Count Your Blessings: Turn to the last several pages of your prayer journal and start a list of "Blessings." Don't stop until you have written down 10 things for which you are thankful to God. Begin to incorporate this discipline of counting your blessings into your quiet times.

In Genesis we read that Eve focused on the one thing she could NOT have (fruit from one tree), rather than being grateful for all those things God had already provided her with. Is there something you don't have right now that you may be putting too much of your focus on? Ask God to show you what may be prohibiting you from being more grateful. Then ask Him to help you release whatever "this" is to him today (and tomorrow, and the next day...)

APPLY IT NOW #6 - COMPLETE BEFORE SESSION SEVEN

Read Chapters 19, 20, and 21. Highlight areas that seem to speak directly to you.

Turn to the *Walking Through Fire* Contents page and read back over each chapter title. Ask yourself: Which of these "tools" do I need to put into practice this week—i.e., spending more time with the Lord? Taking a step of action toward reconciling with someone? Taking a breather and being still? Writing in your journal...?

Record which chapter tool needs your added attention this week:

Chapter _____

Be mindful that this need to place extra time and energy in one area over another may change on a weekly, even daily, basis.

Quiet Time: Use Priscilla Shirer's 5 Ps of Hearing God Through the Bible as you seek to hear from God this week.

1. Position yourself to hear from God. (Find a quiet place void of distractions.)

2. Pore over the passage, and paraphrase the major points. (Read from several translations and write in your own words what the verse is saying.)

3. Pull out the spiritual principles. (Is it a command? Encouragement? Conviction? What does it mean?)

4. Pose the question. (Am I living in such a way that aligns with this scripture? Be silent long enough to hear God.

5. Plan obedience, and pin down the date. (Strategize ways you will be obedient to God. Get some accountability.)

Some great Scripture to consider "poring over" as you apply the 5 P's are: Philippians 4:8, 1 Peter 2:15, Jeremiah 29:11, Deuteronomy 8:2-3, Ecclesiastes 4:9-12, and/or Proverbs 15:13. Make it your goal to spend time in the Word using this technique at least three times this week.

Steer Clear of Negative, Bitter People: Read the following verses that pertain to the consequences of keeping "bad company" and record what you find.

1 Corinthians 15:33

Proverbs 22:24-25

Proverbs 13:20

Regarding your personal use of social media, ask yourself if your time invested there honors God the way you'd like it to. Make the adjustments you need to better honor the Lord with the time you spend on your phone, computer and television. Write down what your goal is this week to improve in this area:

Go Get Your Manna: Unbelief says, "I will not trust what I cannot see." Worrying means we do not believe God can look after the practical details of our lives. Dependence with obedience is the cure for our unbelief. What is something you feel needs to happen in the weeks to come in order to move you forward to the place you believe God wants you to be? It may be in your job, your health, your home, a relationship, your passion. Write down 1-2 steps you can take this week towards making this desire actually happen:

1.

2.

Share Your Weariness: Have you found yourself a prayer partner yet? If not, please do so this week. This is a great place to begin in sharing your weariness. Galatians 6:2 says, *Carry each other's burdens, and in this way you will fulfill the law of Christ.*

Who might you be able to share your burden with this week?

Whose burden might you be able to help carry for them?

If you have found yourself (or at least your emotional self) isolated from others for weeks, stop and pray and ask God to bring you a friend with whom you can share. If God brings someone to mind, then "get out of your tent and go get your manna" (give her a call)!

Plan Something Fun: How are you doing in the "having fun" department? Read back over the "Fun Adventures" listed in the chapter and do a Pick Two which you can do with a friend in the next 1-2 weeks. Consider asking someone in our class to join you. Which two did you choose?

1.

2.

APPLY IT NOW #7 - COMPLETE BEFORE SESSION EIGHT
Read Chapters 22, 23, 24. Highlight areas of particular interest. Write down any questions you have for our last session together.

Do Not Worry Beforehand: Are you someone who prefers to have every word planned out in advance in regards to how you are going to answer someone in a difficult situation? Reread Mark 13:11— *Do not worry about what to say. Just say whatever is given you at the time, for it is not you speaking, but the Holy Spirit.*

Do you believe that God's Spirit (who resides inside of you if you are a follower of Christ) is able to give you the best words to speak in a certain situation? It's what Scripture tells us He can do. So the next time you are needing to say something to someone, take a breath and PRAY and ask God to give you the words to speak. AND give him permission to SHUT your mouth before you say something that does not need to be said.

Write out Mark 13:11 (above) and add it to your Scripture collection. Remember that deciding NOT to worry is a choice you can make. God will help you if you choose to lean into Him in your trial instead of choosing to worry.

Pray for Your Spouse: Read Zechariah 4:6—*Not by might nor by power, but by my spirit, says the Lord Almighty.* Answer this question: How do I pray for my spouse (or my ex) when I don't have it in me to pray?

Decide to lift up your spouse/ex to the Lord four different days this week. Pray for his salvation, repentant heart, release from past patterns of sin. Put a date after each day completed:

1.

2.

3.

4.

Write out 1 Peter 2:5 on 3x5 and work on memorizing the verse—*For it is God's will that by doing good you should silence the ignorant talk of foolish men.* Be encouraged by the NIV note on this verse: "Good citizenship counters false charges made against Christians and thus commends the gospel to unbelievers." Be determined to keep your focus on doing the next "good" thing God would have you do and leave all the hearsay from others and consequences in God's hands.

Write down at least one thing you are pretty certain God is wanting you to wait on before taking a step further in that particular direction:

*This week ask your prayer partner to hold you accountable to wait.

Open up your journal, write today's date and write:

> (Your name), I want you to wait on Me before you
> (write whatever you feel He wants you to wait on Him for).
> Know that I want My best for you.
> —God

> God is a God of clarity. If you don't have it, wait.

Walking On Water: Look back over Matt 14:27-33. As Peter was walking on the water toward Jesus, what happened when he shifted his focus off of Jesus and onto the storm?

List three things you can do to help you not to sink: (Peek at the Table of Contents if you need some hints)

1.

2.

3.

Remember, it IS all about your abiding in Christ. The more time you hang out with Him this week, the better you will get to know Him and ENJOY His company!

If you have been blessed by this book,
Kirby would like to hear your story.

All comments and suggestions can be made at:
kirbyking0413@gmail.com.

To learn more about other resources available from Kirby,
visit her website at: HopeforHardPlaces.com